HEARD BY GOD

SHERYL SUA

ACKNOWLEDGEMENTS

First of all, my deepest thanks to my Father in Heaven for the gift of life. I am indebted to your unconditional love that has seen me through this amazing journey of life so far. I can't wait to see you face to face! Thank you Father for your love, your grace … for carrying us. For hearing my cries, wiping away my tears, understanding my questions and loving me anyway. Thank you for the grace poured on us daily to keep trusting you, to never give up on hope, to keep on loving, and to always offer grace to each other. Thanks for wrapping your arms around me every single day.

Secondly, my darling Michael. Thank you for trusting in and encouraging me to write our story. I knew when we met that I couldn't let you slip out of my life, whatever the cost. You have been *so* worth the wait! Thanks for sticking with me, even in the most challenging of times. I couldn't have made it through without you. Going through this tough chapter of our lives has only made me admire and love you more. Thank you for always loving our Father first, and me second. You have my heart forever.

To my one and only Layla-Grace. Your maturity far exceeds your age, my little lovely. I love you more than words can say and I'm more than thankful that God trusted your Daddy and I with you. I'm sure Sammy is watching from Heaven and is so very proud of you, just like we are. You will always be a big sister, honey.

My family – Dad, Mum, Ric, Marissa, Ronn, Rochelle, Jeff and Eva, Elijah, Ethan, Eden, Arielle and Leah. I'm so very, very proud to call you my family. A person is shaped by the environment they are raised in and you've all shaped me well (wink)! Thank you for your incredible support over the years and especially around Sammy's death. You're always such a source of strength, encouragement, fun, laughter and creativity for me. I'm so grateful for siblings – you guys just "get" me and I love you so! Dad and Mum – thanks for the example you have set, of unshakeable faith. I pray that Michael and I can be such an example to our daughter too. Thanks for an amazing godly heritage!

My in-laws – Dad and Mum, Pona and Tili, Seta and Debs, Richard, Nesa, Meta, Benji, Joshua, Xander, Caleb, Israel, Jordan, Elena, Fa'aesea, Faith, Mikyah and Korde. I love how you always put family first. I love how you gather around whenever any of the family are going through stuff and you're just "there". Words are not necessary when just "being there" shows the love you have for each other. Thanks too for your overwhelming support for us during the time of Sammy's death. You took such great care of our family over that time; your thoughtfulness, generosity, prayers, and hugs supported us so much more than words can ever say. We are beyond grateful for each of you.

Our Beacon Hill Church family – past and present. Thanks for loving us as you have done. For those of you who walked with us through this chapter of our lives when our world was literally shaken, and for sticking by our side and giving us strength. Thank you for all the prayers, hugs, text messages, gifts and dinners during our loss, and for being a "safe place" for us as we journeyed through our grief. It was so great that I could come to Church, even on the days when I didn't feel ok – and know that I would be accepted just as I was. Thank you.

Pastors Luka and Jo Robertson, you came into our lives at such a crucial time in our journey. Thank you for walking with us through this season and for "adopting" us into the Hope Centre family! We love you both so much.

Pastors Mike and Jeannie Knott. You have been a part of my life now for nearly 30 years (goodness! Where has the time gone?). Thanks for always speaking life over me and setting such an amazing example of a life well lived with Jesus at the centre. And thank you for writing the foreword for this book; I couldn't think of anyone I would rather have had write it.

Krystee Craig. What can I say. Thanks to you for confirming our son's name! This was the best gift you could ever have given us. For this and your friendship, I am eternally grateful.

All of our friends who messaged us, prayed for us, and called us – I would love nothing more than to mention each of you by name, but I'm worried I may miss someone. There are so many of you, and spread out all across the world! If we could have, Michael and I would have loved to send every single one of you a gift to say thanks for loving us and just "being there" for us. But please take this as our sincerest gratitude for all your encouragement, well-wishes, condolences, Bible verses, prayers, dinners, cards, gifts and flowers. And thanks too for helping me decide on a title and cover for this book! No man (or woman!) is an island and we are truly thankful for each of you.

Rachel Nankivell of Heartfelt Photography – thank you SO much for your gift. The photos you took of our son are like gold to us. You captured Sammy and our family so beautifully, and we are eternally grateful for these memories.

Finally, if any of the medical team that worked with us from the hospital are reading this – you have our heartfelt thanks. Thank you for doing your very best for us and Sammy. We appreciate you more than you will ever know. Thank you for going the extra mile for us; we know that your hearts were broken too. We pray that God continues to use your gifts and talents to bring life and healing to so many who need it. May God bless you!

CONTENTS

FOREWORD

It has been a huge privilege to read this book before it goes to print.

It is a very challenging story, that makes one not only appreciate the courage it has taken for Sheryl to pen these words in the midst of her grief, but even more to come to an even greater realisation of the amazing grace of God for those who will reach out in faith and receive it.

Sheryl and her husband Michael have demonstrated, and continue to show, how walking through tragedy with Jesus by your side, and a confidence in the Words He has spoken, can be perhaps the most powerful testimony of character being shaped on the anvil of suffering. Their readiness to forgive, and express love for those who have been accidentally involved in causing their grief, is a miracle, only to be seen through those with a true depth of faith, and an intimate relationship with their Saviour.

May you be challenged and inspired, as we truly have, as you read and absorb this story, and gain strength for things you may be going though right now, or whatever life may bring your way.

Thank you, Sheryl, for sharing your heart. May you and Michael, and beautiful Layla-Grace continue to know God's constant presence in your lives.

Pastors Mike and Jeannie Knott

INTRODUCTION

I have always wanted to write a book. I always thought I would write a series of children's books or maybe a home interiors or some other kind of non-fiction book. Not in a million years did I ever think I would be writing a book about my son Samuel; about the months before his birth, his short life here on earth and the months since his passing.

I had actually started writing a book in early 2016, but didn't feel it was quite the right topic. So, I put it aside and asked God what I should be writing about. I feel that He has answered my question and literally given me a story to write. So here it is.

Our journey has been unbelievable in so many ways, and I knew from the day of Sammy's death, that we really needed to share it. Yes, it is a sad story, but it is also one of hope, grace and God's immeasurable love.

I'm writing this book because I feel someone out there — or maybe a few someone's — could be encouraged by my family's story. To know that through complete tragedy, there is always hope. And that God's grace can help you to get through, one day at a time — just as we have been experiencing. God has never been more real to me and my family as He has been over the past seven months.

I'm also writing this as a way of processing everything that has happened. I'm still broken and on a journey of healing, myself. There have been many, many tears shed during the writing of this book, but also moments of awe at how God became so real to us during this time. By writing our story, I pray God's love washes over me anew and awakens me again to the greatest love that has ever existed. Because love is not a feeling or an emotion – love is a person. And His name is Jesus.

I pray that whomever you are, and whatever situation life has you in right now, that this love finds you and carries you through, also.

"Then, by constantly using your faith, the life of Christ will be released deep inside you, and the resting place of His love will become the very source and root of your life. Then you will be empowered to discover what every holy one experiences – the great magnitude of the astonishing love of Christ in all its dimensions. How deeply intimate and far-reaching is His love! How enduring and inclusive it is! **Endless love beyond measurement that transcends our understanding** – this extravagant love pours into you until you are filled to overflowing with the fullness of God!"[1]

---

[1] Ephesians 3:17-19, The Passion Translation

*The Lord
is my shepherd,
I have all
that I need.*

Psalm 23:1

(New Living Translation)

ONE

It was 20 July 2017, and my husband Michael, and I, were attending the Arise Conference in Wellington. Pastor John Cameron was talking about giving, and I remembered the $200 in my wallet that someone had given us a few weeks earlier. I was holding onto it as I knew that soon we would be needing every penny. Michael's contract with his workplace was ending on 1 September and would not be renewed. He had been applying for other jobs but nothing had come about as yet.

Previously, when his contracts were coming to an end, I would start to worry. He was our main income earner; I worked only two days a week. As he was pastoring a church, he was also receiving an income from them. However, because it was just a small congregation, the income was only enough to cover our phone and power bills.

We were due to go on holiday to Singapore and Indonesia with our 4-year old daughter in a couple of days. Had we known when we booked our flights that his job would be ending, we probably would have cancelled it. It didn't seem the wisest thing to go traipsing around overseas on holiday when one's source of income was about to end, with no promise of anything to come!

So, here we were, sitting in the service listening to Pastor John's offering message, and I felt very challenged. I whispered to Michael who was sitting beside me, "I've still got that money in my wallet."

He whispered back, "how much do you want to give?"

Fighting the desperate urge to cling onto it, I replied, "all of it."

He nodded, and as the offering buckets came around, I put all $200 in. Deep down, I knew we were going to be entering a season where God wanted us to trust Him completely as our Source. So, as I put the money into the bucket, I whispered in my heart, "God, you know we are going to need money. I'm putting this into the bucket as a symbol that we trust You fully. We don't trust money, nor do we trust our employers; You are our Source and we know that You will look after us."

I was holding onto that verse in the Bible that says, "Test me in this, says the Lord Almighty, and see if I will not throw open the floodgates of Heaven and pour out so much blessing that there will not be room enough to store it."[2] We didn't know how God was going to provide for us, but we both had a strong sense that God wanted us to just trust Him - to really trust Him to provide for us.

Three days later, we were on a plane, heading to Singapore. Our family enjoys the tradition of heading somewhere warmer when it is winter in New Zealand, so we were really looking forward to some heat! I was 20 weeks pregnant, and very much looking forward to having a bit of a break and putting my feet up before the baby's arrival.

I'd had my 20-week scan earlier that week and had hoped to confirm the baby's gender, but unfortunately baby was such a wriggler that it was difficult to tell! The person who conducted the scan told us it was probably more likely to be a girl. I was a little disappointed as I had really wanted a son, as had Michael. But our daughter, Layla-Grace, had insisted she was going to have a baby sister. I kept my hopes up that it could still be a boy, but reminded myself that the gender didn't matter whatsoever, as long as our baby was healthy.

---

[2] Malachi 3:10, New International Version

A couple of hours after the scan, my midwife had called me to let me know that the scan had revealed I had a low-lying placenta ("placenta previa"). She didn't think it would be an issue for me to travel, but had called a doctor at the hospital to check this. The doctor had confirmed I would be fine to travel. My midwife advised that if I experienced any bleeding at all during my time overseas, I was to see a doctor – or at least visit a medical centre – immediately. She didn't think this would happen but thought it best to let me know, just in case. I was thankful for her advice, but deep down I didn't think it would apply to me. I hung up and thought, "Whew! At least they didn't stop me from going on holiday!"

We had a lovely time in hot, humid Singapore and then flew to Indonesia to stay with my parents for a few days. My sister, both brothers and I were all born in Central Java, Indonesia. We had moved to New Zealand at different times, to finish our tertiary education. I had left home at the age of 16, but had always made the effort to return to Indonesia every two years or so, whenever possible. I love Indonesia and especially my home-town of Tawangmangu; a small town by Indonesian standards! It is a settlement on the side of a sprawling mountain, about 3,000 metres above sea level. The majority of the locals are vegetable growers or support the local tourist industry, by way of maintaining holiday homes owned by the wealthy who live in the big cities. Because of its' location, the temperature in Tawangmangu is about 25 degrees Celsius on average. This was why many of the locals in hotter cities had holiday homes here; it was lovely and cool. To me, it was just perfect!

I had been so looking forward to coming back to where my parents live, at the Tawangmangu Bible College which they were previously the directors of. My grandparents Dal and Dorothy Walker, had founded this college back in the 1970's, and since that time, there have been thousands of graduates spread across the whole country. Countless numbers of them are pastoring or have started various ministries around Indonesia. The impact that this Bible College has had around the country is huge! My parents were now retired from their role as directors and are now part of the oversight. As much as my siblings and I have encouraged them to retire to New Zealand where their children and grandkids live, their hearts are dedicated 100% to the work that they do there. I honour them for that. Their passion for God and people is inspiring.

So, we arrived in Tawangmangu after a lovely four days in Singapore but unfortunately, Layla-Grace came down with a severe temperature that day. We took her to see the local doctor and he diagnosed her with having Typhus Salmonella, a type of bug which one contracts from food or water. We guessed she may have picked it up while in Singapore playing in an outdoor water fountain. The doctor looked at me and asked how many months I was into my pregnancy, and I told him 6. He asked me if I was well and I said I was. He kept looking at me while checking Layla-Grace, but didn't say anything more. It happened that a few months later, when my mother went back to see him for a check-up, he admitted to her that he thought there was something a little "off" with the way I looked and had been concerned about my pregnancy.

He wasn't the only person on this holiday who seemed a little concerned for my well-being.

Some other people also asked how my pregnancy was and advised me to be sure not to lift anything heavy and to get plenty of rest. To be honest, I felt a bit annoyed at these comments. I wasn't used to having people be overly concerned with my well-being! This was my second pregnancy, and the first had gone without a hitch so of course this one would be fine too, I told myself. I wondered whether perhaps in Indonesia, people were a lot more cautious during pregnancy than they were in the Western world?

Layla-Grace was prescribed some medication and spent the rest of the week in Tawangmangu just resting. She recovered just in time for our flight to Bali. We had invited my parents to come on holiday with us and were all so looking forward to it. The night before we left for Bali, I felt incredibly uncomfortable. My belly felt huge as though I was already nine months into my pregnancy! I really hoped that this was just a temporary thing; I couldn't imagine feeling this way (and getting bigger) over the next 18 weeks!

That night as I slept, I had a dream that it was the next morning and we were departing for Bali. In my dream, we had just arrived and soon after descending from the plane, I started to bleed. It was a significant amount, so I raced off to the hospital with my Dad. Upon arrival, they gave me a thorough examination and scanned me twice. I don't remember much more of the dream after that.

When I woke up, I put my hand on my belly and was relieved to discover that it was just a dream. Thank goodness! I was also over the moon to find that the discomfort I had felt the previous night was mostly gone. We flew from Central Java with my parents and arrived in Bali on schedule. We were met at the airport by a lovely lady, Lina, a member of the church where my Dad would be speaking the next day, Sunday. Lina drove us to the hotel where the church was putting us up for the night. The next day we would transfer over to the hotel that I had booked us all into for our family holiday.

As I was standing and waiting for Lina to check us into the hotel, I suddenly felt a gush of blood, just as I had experienced in my dream the night before. I didn't say anything to anyone, but as soon as we got into our bedroom, I raced for the bathroom. I panicked when I saw the amount of blood; there was a lot more than could be considered normal during pregnancy. I collected myself by saying that everything would be okay and that the midwife had warned me this could be possible. I just knew I needed to get to a doctor ASAP.

I told Michael, who suggested perhaps he come with me and leave Layla-Grace with Mum and Dad at the hotel. I knocked on my parents' room next door and told them what had happened and that Michael and I were planning to get a taxi to the nearby hospital. As I was preparing to go, Mum came back to our room and told me that she and Dad would come with me because Dad wanted to get a check-up (he had been having some stomach problems).

So, exactly as I had dreamed, within an hour of arriving in Bali - I experienced bleeding and went to the hospital with my dad! I'm not exactly sure why I had that dream, but I think that perhaps God wanted to give me a "heads-up", because He loves me and didn't want me to worry.

I did worry though. When we arrived at the hospital, I went to the receptionist and had to choke back tears as I told her in Indonesian what had happened. She pointed me to the emergency department and told me to go there right away.

As I lay on the bed waiting to be seen, I placed my hands on my tummy and prayed repeatedly that baby would be okay. I cried silently as I worried what may happen. But I reminded myself that God had everything under control and that all would work out fine. The staff were very thorough (again, as per my dream!) and after asking many questions and doing various tests, I was sent to have a scan. I couldn't wait to see my baby again and for Mum to have the chance to see her youngest grandchild for the first time too! Oh, the love I felt as I saw my little one wriggling away inside my tummy. This baby was definitely a *lot* more active than Layla-Grace had ever been. "Oh dear," I thought, "I'll most certainly be kept on my feet with this one!"

The obstetrician, Doctor Agus[3], conducted a very thorough scan. He advised me that the placenta was nowhere near the cervix; it was no longer low-lying, and had moved upwards. This was good news for me, as it meant I could still have a natural birth. This would not be possible if the placenta remained low-lying, as

---

[3] Name changed to protect privacy

it would mean the baby would be delivered after the placenta. Of course, this would have serious implications on the newborn.

Doctor Agus confirmed that everything was well with the baby and could only presume the bleeding was perhaps caused by a turbulent flight or rough landing. I didn't think we had experienced either, but was just relieved to hear that my baby was fine. Doctor Agus also told me that I had been having contractions. How had I not realised this? But as I thought back to the previous night when I felt so uncomfortable, I realized I had indeed been contracting. After all, I guess it had been four years since I had last felt contractions! He prescribed some Duvadilan tablets to help ease them, and was especially concerned if they should happen during our flights back to New Zealand. I was advised to keep the tablets in my pocket, just in case.

He also told me that I should limit my walking and that I must have bed rest for the duration of our time in Bali. I sighed. Oh well, at least we were here for a holiday, and thankfully, Michael had insisted on booking a villa with our own private pool. The man has insight, let me tell you!

I grabbed the opportunity to ask Doctor Agus if he could see what gender the baby was. After moving the scan this way and that, he said, "70% chance of being a boy." Oh, the joy! I was so over the moon. "Thank you, Jesus," I whispered, breathing a sigh of relief. He had heard our prayer. I knew the doctor had not said 100%, but in my heart, I knew it was a boy. All the worry, anxiety and fear I had experienced in the last few hours faded away. We were having a son. And I was so very pleased that Mum had been there to see him and be the first to hear the news with me. A few moments later, we met Dad in the foyer of the hospital and I proudly announced that we were having a son. He smiled, put his hand on my shoulder and told me to, "look after little Sam."

After being gone for about four hours, we returned to the hotel just as Michael was just putting Layla-Grace to sleep. I was bursting to tell them the exciting news that baby was a boy! Layla-Grace wasn't so pleased about having a brother because she had always insisted that she was having a baby sister. But Michael was thrilled. We spent the next hour or so, using all our persuasive powers, trying to convince Layla-Grace of the benefits of having a little brother.

For the next four days in Bali, I rested as much as possible. We did leave the hotel a couple of times, but both times I used a wheelchair to get around. Layla-Grace thought this was incredibly fun and did her best to push around me in it.

Thankfully, our flights back home were uneventful and I experienced no contractions. I was thoroughly exhausted though, and even managed to doze off while sitting upright — a bit of a miracle for me!

The day after we arrived home, Saturday, 12 August, I sent a text message to my midwife telling her what had happened and that the contractions had since eased off. She didn't seem concerned, and replied by text message to say that we would have another scan at 32 weeks to see the position of the placenta. I was surprised at her short reply and the non-concerned tone, but figured she knew better than me. So, I pushed it all aside and went back to life as normal.

I leave
the gift of peace
with you -
my peace.

John 14:27

(The Passion Translation)

TWO

Wednesday, 13 September

Michael's contract had ended on 1 September, and he was now spending most of his days at home applying for jobs. I was working two days a week as the finance and office administrator at an early childhood centre. Our income had drastically reduced over the last two weeks and we were starting to feel the pressure.

Baby boy was due in twelve weeks and I knew that if Michael started a job soon, he wouldn't likely be entitled to parental leave. I wasn't quite sure how I would manage having a newborn and caring for a four-year-old, all on my own. But despite the mounting pressure, deep down inside I knew that God had our back. He had never let us down in the past and I knew He would not let us down now. Somehow, things would work out, even if I couldn't see how.

As always, I was looking forward to my midwife visit. On this particular morning, Layla-Grace didn't seem her usual self, but she needed to come with me anyway because she attended the childcare centre where I worked.

Lara[4], my midwife, had not been available at several of my previous visits, so I had been seen by someone else on her team. Today though, it was nice to finally catch up with her. I briefed her about what had happened in Bali and she reiterated that we would have the scan at 32 weeks' gestation to see if the placenta had moved. If not, then baby would have to be delivered by caesarean section. Since coming back from Indonesia, I had experienced a few contractions. One evening in particular I had not even able to finish washing the dishes because of the discomfort. I told Lara about this, but also that I hadn't been pushing myself, and the contractions appeared to have eased off in recent days.

We heard baby boy's strong heartbeat and Lara commented on how active he was. On previous occasions, it had been hard for the midwife on duty to find his heartbeat because he moved around so much! This was possibly also due to the fact that the placenta was positioned in the front of my abdomen and baby would have been behind it.

---

[4] Name changed to protect privacy

All was well with me, too. My blood pressure was normal and I had no swelling in my feet or hands. The only thing that we didn't get to check that morning was a urine sample because Layla-Grace and I were rushing to get to the appointment and ran out of time to do this before seeing Lara. Neither Lara nor I were too worried about it, as everything else appeared to be fine.

At work, I got busy typing and retyping my desk file. This was a set of instructions for how to do my job, which I would give to the person who would be filling in while I was on maternity leave. For some strange reason, over the past two days I had felt a very pressing need to update it as quickly as I could. I had a very strong sense that baby would be born early. My guess was about three weeks early. I also felt like we needed to be getting the cot set up soon — and all the other baby paraphernalia — sooner rather than later.

During the course of the day, my lower back and right leg started to feel awfully uncomfortable. Because I sit for many hours of the day, I dismissed the pains as typical pregnancy aches and thought that I just needed to get up and move around a bit more.

At the end of my work day, I went next door to collect Layla-Grace. The poor little darling had tears streaming down her cheeks and was being carried by Lucy,[5] one of her teachers.

Lucy told me that Layla-Grace had been unwell for most of the day; she had even had a nap, which was unlike her. I cuddled her up into my arms, felt her very warm forehead and then left for home. I had planned to visit a fabric store on the way home in order to buy fabric pieces to make baby's quilt, but decided it could wait for another week. Layla-Grace was too unwell. I drove straight home and she climbed into bed immediately.

We kept an eye on her as she slept that night. Her temperature was still very high, but she took some Paracetamol and seemed to do okay after that.

I wasn't feeling too tired, so after I got into bed, I trawled the internet looking for different versions of songs that we could do for our Christmas service. Baby was due on Tuesday, 5 December, and I knew that I wouldn't be able to do much soon after he was born. So, I thought I would get the ball rolling early so that it wasn't left to the last minute. I finally turned my light out at around 11:30 pm, and Michael was already snoring beside me.

---

[5] Name changed to protect privacy

Thursday, 14 September

I woke up in the morning and reached for my phone to read the devotions for the day. Today was day three of a plan entitled, "100 Names of God," and the reading was entitled, "Jehovah Shalom – The Lord is Peace." A passage jumped out at me, "True peace – what the Bible calls 'Shalom' – is much more than just the absence of strife. Shalom isn't merely the absence of conflict; it's also the presence of fullness and joy, friendship and love."

I was in the middle of reading John 14:27,[6] when Layla-Grace woke up and came into our room. She crawled into bed between Michael and I and asked what my Bible said. I read aloud the verses to her and then prayed that God would pour His peace over our whole day, whatever we would get up to. This day.

Looking back now, I realise the significance of what seemed a completely insignificant moment.

Normally today, Layla-Grace would be attending her other daycare centre, just up the road from our house. We were transitioning her out of the childcare centre where I worked, because once baby was born I would not be driving all the way

---

[6] "I leave the gift of peace with you — my peace. Not the kind of fragile peace given by the world, but my perfect peace. Don't yield to fear or be troubled in your hearts — instead, be courageous!"- Passion Translation

into the city just to drop her off and pick her up. Today would have been Layla-Grace's fifth day at Lifestart, but because she hadn't been well, we decided it best to keep her at home.

I was slightly annoyed at this change of plan because I had a long, growing list of things that I wanted to get done before baby arrived. We needed to get Layla-Grace's old baby items out of storage, and I really wanted to make our baby boy a quilt. I had nearly finished making a mobile to hang above his bed, and wanted to complete it. Then of course was all the washing that needed to be done: bedding, clothes and so on. But my little girl was sick, so all those things would just have to wait another day.

Around 10:15am, Michael went for a run and Layla-Grace was playing in the living room. I was sitting at the desk near her, typing up words for a new song that the band would be rehearsing tonight. I was also trying to memorise the words, as I would be leading it in Church this Sunday!

I finished typing the lyrics and told Layla-Grace that I would get her a little bowl of munchies for morning tea. As I stood up from the desk, immediately a gush of blood came out, running down my legs. I froze. This was a familiar feeling, but a lot more blood this time. Keeping calm, I told Layla-Grace that I was just going to the bathroom and that I would get her morning tea in a minute.

Heart panicking, I got to the toilet as quickly as I could. Another gush of blood. This was more than what I had lost in Bali. Layla-Grace could hear me making gasping sounds, and came to see what was going on. Trying to keep my composure, I quickly made a plan. I asked her to leave the bathroom and reminded her that I would get morning tea shortly. I told her that everything was okay.

By the time Michael came back from his run, about 10 minutes later, I had cleaned up and had just finished talking to the midwife on the phone. He walked in to, "Hon, I'm going to the hospital. I've been bleeding again." I insisted on driving myself, thinking it would only be a short visit, but reconsidered and took up his offer to drop me off. "Just in case you're there for a while. I may need the car." I agreed.

We left immediately and drove to our local hospital, just a few minutes away from our home. I prayed silently in my head the whole way, and grasped Michael's free hand tightly. Words were not needed. I didn't want my fear to show, especially in front of Layla-Grace. Michael asked if I wanted them both to accompany me, but I said they could just drop me off. I wasn't sure how long this would take. He asked me to keep him posted and that he would come back as soon as I needed him. Feeling incredibly afraid, I gave them both a kiss, got out of the car and quickly made my way to the maternity ward.

Lara arrived about two minutes after me and she showed me straight to the delivery suite. We chatted for a bit and then suddenly the room was full of people. Some were checking my blood pressure, some asking questions, and others inserting needles and lines into my arms. I was told that my blood pressure reading was very high. This was very unusual for me as I'm usually on the low side.

The doctor on duty at the time asked me who had given the "go-ahead" for travel to Indonesia and Singapore. I told her that Lara had called the hospital to get the all-clear. The doctor replied, "I never would have given you the go-ahead!"

The medical staff gave me a dose of magnesium sulphate, which I was told was to assist with baby's brain development, in case he was to arrive early. Some months later I read that it helps to prevent brain injury from lack of oxygen, and assists with prolonging pregnancy for up to two days[7]. Another thing I didn't realise till the time of writing this book, is that magnesium sulphate is also used to reduce the risk of seizures in women who suffer from pre-eclampsia. "Pre-eclampsia is a pregnancy

---

[7] www.healthline.com

complication that causes high blood pressure, kidney and lung damage and other issues. Women who have pre-eclampsia have a high level of protein in their urine and also have swelling in their feet, legs and hands."[8]

They also gave me a steroid injection, which I was told helps speed up the development of baby's lungs and gut, among other things. Just in case he was to arrive early.

I had it in my mind that baby wouldn't be arriving anytime soon, and that this would be a short visit to the hospital and then I would go home again. So, I was completely surprised when they decided it would be best to send me in the ambulance to another hospital, in case baby did come early. His gestation was now 28 weeks and 2 days. Our local hospital did not have the facilities to care for a premature baby.

At this point, Lara called Michael to tell him what was happening and that I was being transferred to a different hospital. He and Layla-Grace returned immediately.

There was quite a negotiation that took place to have me transferred to the other hospital. They were more than at capacity; there weren't enough beds! In the end, the hospitals did a patient exchange in order to make room for me.

---

[8] www.webmd.com

By 1 pm, I was being strapped into a stretcher by the ambulance staff and wheeled out to the waiting ambulance. I was still feeling very afraid of the unknown and how quickly everything was happening, but I didn't want Layla-Grace to worry. So, I gave her a huge grin from my stretcher and explained excitedly how Mummy was going for a ride in the ambulance with all the lights on and sirens blaring! She managed a brave smile but my heart broke that I couldn't stay and give her a huge cuddle.

Meanwhile, Michael had arranged for his sister, Deborah, to come collect Layla-Grace and take her back to her home. He would follow me to the hospital in our car.

On the way there, the paramedic asked me if I did yoga. I wondered if this was out of admiration for my incredibly toned-looking body … but I knew that could most certainly *not* be the reason! I'm about the most unfit person on the planet. "No, I don't. Why?" I asked.

"You're very calm! Most pregnant women we take in the ambulance would be very stressed by now."

Aha. I felt like saying, "Buddy, I do something *way* better than yoga; it's called prayer." I didn't. But I suddenly remembered the devotions I had read that morning about Jehovah Shalom – God our peace. And I realised that God my peace, was right there with me in that moment, despite the fearful situation.

We arrived at the hospital at around 1:20 pm, and I was met by Doctor Jack[9] who was absolutely lovely and helped me to relax immediately. He conducted a scan right away to check baby's situation. My little baby was flipping around as always. Such an active little man. They also pumped more magnesium sulphate into me, which made me feel very hot.

Michael arrived soon after and I filled him in on what had happened. The doctors had asked me not to eat or drink anything, in case I had to go into surgery. At around 3 pm, contractions started and were coming every 2-3 minutes. My cervix wasn't dilating however, so I was not going into labour. By about 4:30 pm, the contractions had eased back and the bleeding had also completely stopped. The hospital team had discovered a blood clot which they thought was on the edge of the placenta. Their concern was that if the clot was from behind the placenta, this could mean a placental abruption. In other words, the placenta detaching from the wall of the uterus. When this happens, baby's supply of oxygen and nutrients are affected. However, they seemed confident that it was on the edge of the placenta, not in the back of it.

---

[9] Name changed to protect privacy

Around this time, Michael started contacting family and close friends to ask them to please pray.

The team who were looking after me were constantly checking my blood pressure, which apparently was still very high. I was asked several times whether I had a headache or pains in my abdominal region. They also asked if I had blurred vision. I didn't have any of these symptoms. A younger doctor on duty came in and checked my reflexes. I didn't know what this was all about. I was sure I had reasonably good reflexes.

I didn't realise till later, that pre-eclampsia can cause unusually active reflexes. Incredibly high blood pressure can eventuate in uncontrollable seizures. Severe pre-eclampsia can result in death, caused by extreme blood pressure in the head, burst blood vessels in the brain, ruptured liver, retinal detachment and kidney failure.

Of course, I didn't know all this at the time. I just knew something was horribly wrong, that my blood pressure was very high and I was extremely concerned for my baby and my own health. I was also ridiculously thirsty.

By around 5 or 6 pm that day, I was having visions of the biggest glass of water imaginable, filled with lemon, mint and ice cubes! I hadn't had lunch that day either, only a handful of almonds that I had put in my bag as I dashed out the door to the hospital that morning. I was finally given a cup of ice cubes to help quench my thirst. Never have I appreciated ice cubes so much before!

That evening, my brother-in-law Ric Knott, came to see Michael and I. Ric is married to my sister Marissa and together they pastor a thriving local Church. I was *so* grateful for him. As he prayed for me, I felt God's incredible peace surround us in that room. He told us that their church was praying for us. I realised then that we were surrounded by prayers. Family, our congregation, friends, colleagues, acquaintances, people in our neighbourhood, city and even around the world! How grateful I was that regardless of time and space, our prayers are heard by Heaven. Just knowing that we had so much support out there was something I clung to. Community is so important! Having others stand with us when we were in complete uncertainty brought us such encouragement and strength.

Not long after Ric left that evening, my younger brother Jeff came to visit. Jeff is awesome. He gives the best hugs and always has such a happy disposition. They say the youngest child is usually the most easy-going. They sure got that right about Jeff!

Around 10 pm, the contractions had picked up again, coming every 2 - 4 minutes. The medical team wondered whether the contractions were being brought on by the blood clot which was shedding. The cervix was still not dilating and therefore I was not going into labour. Baby's heartbeat was strong and he was as active as always.

They decided to give me a second steroid injection and keep the magnesium sulphate dripping into me. By this time, I began to wonder if things may just become steady and I would be released to go home. I had heard talk earlier of the possibility of letting me go, however, it would mean being released back to my local hospital for bed rest until baby was born. I wasn't sure I liked that scenario!

I despise needles and have always been terrified of surgery, so I would have loved to have been released, but at the same time, I was thinking that, "perhaps now that we're here, we could just get this over and done with." I couldn't bear the thought of having to come again in about eight weeks or so, just to do this over!

The contractions eased at around 10:30 pm or thereabouts, but soon after, I started shaking uncontrollably. When the midwife on duty checked me and couldn't find out what was wrong, I realised I was having a panic attack. I had to tell myself, "I've got this! I *can* do this!" and I calmed down. I remembered a book I had read a few months earlier by Dr Caroline Leaf,[10] about the brain. It is wired in such a way that you actually can control fears, worries, etc., by changing the negative thoughts going through it. I had to speak words of encouragement to change the negative tune playing in my head. I knew that if I could control my brain, my body would follow suit. I quoted Bible verses over and over to myself too, to remind me that God was with me and that He was in control of all that was going on. Verses such as, "I can do all things through Christ who strengthens me,"[11] and, "The peace of God which surpasses all understanding, will guard your hearts and minds through Christ Jesus." [12]

Jehovah Shalom – God my peace, was still with me, through all of this. Even through my anxiety attack, He was with me and holding my hand.

---

[10] https://drleaf.com
[11] Philippians 4:13, New King James version
[12] Philippians 4:7, New King James version

Even though I walk
through the
darkest valley,
I will fear no evil,
for You are with me;
Your rod and Your staff,
they comfort me.

Psalm 23:4

(New International Version)

THREE

Friday, 15 September

Sometime around mid-morning on Friday, I was finally allowed to have some food and water to drink. I was told that I would be able to eat and drink at mealtimes, but no snacking in between just in case I had to be raced into surgery. I devoured my breakfast!

Another scan had been scheduled for 11 am that morning, so I was looking forward to seeing my little baby and finding out how he was doing. During the scan, Michael and I noticed that baby was not his usual active self. In fact, the sonographer was able to show us the profile of baby's face, which we had never been able to see previously. Baby was lying rather still, which made me feel very worried and upset. We asked the sonographer if he could confirm baby's gender and he told us it was 80% certain that baby was a boy. He printed a couple of pictures of baby's face and we were interested to see that the profile of his face looked very different to Layla-Grace's. We couldn't wait to see what he looked like in person!

I was taken back to my room to rest. I hadn't slept very well the night before. The staff had been in and out every hour to check baby's heartbeat and to monitor my blood pressure too. Of course, I was very grateful that they did, but it just meant that I was now rather sleep deprived. Michael had also put on some music to create a peaceful atmosphere in our room. I thought it would be a good idea to help calm my nerves, but in actual fact, I don't sleep very well with noise – even relaxing music.

We met a new midwife who was on duty for the weekend. Joelle[13] was marvelous. She was one of those people who make you feel completely at ease in their presence; she had a fantastic sense of sarcastic humour but was also incredibly caring.

Jeff came to visit again in the afternoon to keep me company. Michael took the opportunity to head home for a shower and also to see Layla-Grace, who was staying with my parents in-law and Michael's sister's family. Poor little girl must have been rather confused from the chaos the day before at the hospital.

---

[13] Name changed to protect privacy

Her Aunty Deborah had picked her up, brought her back to our house to pack some things, then taken her home.

Later that evening while Michael was still out, Jeff left and my sister Marissa came to visit. She had been aching to come earlier, but had been busy with the kids and other family routines. We called my parents via FaceTime and I recall telling them that the bleeding and contractions had completely stopped. My Mum, amazing woman of faith that she is, believed that the worst was over and things would now start to improve. Marissa and I looked at each other at that point, both quite aware that my baby and I were nowhere out of the dark just yet. There was just a sense that I wasn't going to be leaving the hospital anytime soon and that this situation could take a turn for the worst at any minute.

Before she left, Marissa prayed for me. Once again, I was reminded that we were not alone. Our prayers have power because God promises that He hears us when we pray: "The eyes of the Lord watch over those who do right and His ears are open to their prayers."[14]

I felt a real peace wash over me, as I remembered that God was in control of everything. Even before I was born, He knew all the

---

[14] 1 Peter 3:12

days of my life, and there wasn't one thing He wasn't in control of.

Michael returned from visiting Layla-Grace, bringing a few necessary items that we hadn't been able to pack before coming to hospital. As the evening drew into night and the night wore on, Joelle's shift ended and Jane[15] came on as my midwife. She came in very frequently during the night, becoming very concerned at baby's lack of movement, suggesting baby may need to be delivered very soon.

Michael and I realized then that we hadn't quite settled on a name for the baby! We had tossed up the names Arden, Samuel and Jonathan but hadn't quite agreed on anything yet. Many months earlier, Michael had suggested the name Samuel if baby was a boy. I had never liked the name much, despite the fact that it has a great meaning and was also my Dad's first name! A few days later, rather out of the blue, Layla-Grace said to me, "Mummy, what if we call baby, Samuel?" I was rather taken back because she hadn't even been in the room when Michael had suggested it to me!

I remembered back to when we were in Bali and my Dad had said, "You have to look after little Sam." I thought it was odd

---

[15] Name changed to protect privacy

that this name was being mentioned again, but had brushed it off, thinking Dad was just suggesting a namesake.

Back to present day. Earlier that evening, on 15 September, Michael had received a text message from some pastor friends of ours. Krystee wrote that she had been praying for us and for baby. She wrote that every time she prayed for us, the name "Samuel" kept coming to mind. She wasn't sure if the name had any significance to us at all, but just thought she would write and tell us anyway.

As Michael read out Krystee's message, we both started crying. I had always felt that this child's name would be very important and that I couldn't just choose any name I wished, as strange as that may sound. I had been praying for months that God would help us choose the right name for him. Michael and I believe that a person's name shapes who they are and who they become, and I really felt more than anything that God had to tell us what to name him. I knew God already had a name for our son, and I had been asking Him to tell me what it was.

Krystee's message was all the confirmation I needed. Michael and I agreed on naming our son Samuel Jonathan Sua. Samuel is a Hebrew name from the Bible, which means "name of God" "asked of God" and "heard by God." Jonathan is also a Hebrew name from the Bible which means "the Lord gave" or "the Lord of giving."[16] We loved how the meaning of both these names went together really well. We had asked God for a son, He heard and had given.

After deciding on the name, I tried to settle in and get some sleep. I couldn't. Michael told me not to worry and to try and get some sleep, but how could I when my baby's movements were abnormally quiet, and I was facing imminent surgery? One of – if not *the* – greatest fears of my life! I admired Michael's ability to sleep soundly through the night on the chair in the room.

Sometime around 11 pm, Jane came into the room with Doctor Elaine.[17] Elaine was one of the surgeons on duty. She told me that she had been monitoring the readings of baby's movements and that they were quite concerned at his lack of activity. Elaine also told me that they had decided it was best to have surgery to get him out. She needed to check first with the senior surgeon on duty, Dennis,[18] to obtain his recommendations, and then would take it from there. She left, but a few minutes later Elaine returned to confirm we were scheduled for surgery at 1 am.

---

[16] www.abarim-publications.com
[17] Name changed to protect privacy
[18] Name changed to protect privacy

I started to panic. I did not feel one bit ready for surgery. I didn't even feel ready to have baby yet. Nothing was ready for him at home, and I wasn't mentally prepared to be a mum of a newborn again just yet. In my head, I still had about 12 weeks to go till his due date of 5 December! But more than anything, I was terrified of surgery. I hate needles at the best of times, but to have a knife cut me open, that is one of the things I've feared most, all my life.

However, if this was best for baby, I would need to bite the bullet and endure it, so to speak. We had to get him out right away. Jane advised me not to worry, and that this type of surgery was the maternity unit's "bread and butter"; they conducted these surgeries all the time. I knew it would all be okay and had to tell myself I could do this.

Over the next hour, various people came to see me to sign pieces of paper. They explained that an early arrival (28 weeks and 4 days) could possibly mean slow development, risk of cerebral palsy, and hearing and eye impairment among other things.

Michael awoke in the midst of all the commotion. When I told him that our little baby boy was going to be born, he smiled with excitement. I asked him what the date was, and he replied 15 September. The time of surgery was scheduled for 1 am, which would mean that our Sammy's birthday would be 16 September.

We looked at each other excitedly, realising that we would be meeting our son very soon!

We met Dr Dena,[19] who introduced herself as a consultant neonatologist in the neonatal intensive care unit. She explained what would happen after our son was delivered and how the neonatal team would take over from that point. She reassured us both, telling us that the success rate of delivering a baby at seven months was the same as that of a nine-month old. She also told us that Sam would have to stay in the unit for several weeks or until he was ready to be released and come home with us.

I was prepped and then wheeled into surgery.

The fear in me caused my shoulders and neck to become ridiculously tense. I had to keep telling my brain to relax them. But they would tense right back up. In hindsight, it took maybe four days or more for that tension in my shoulders to really let go. In the next few days, even as I lay recuperating, they would automatically tighten back up. It was difficult to sleep because of the tension.

The entire surgery team were amazing. As we entered the room, everything was abuzz. They briefed Michael and I about what was going to happen, and then got me ready.

---

[19] Name changed to protect privacy

During the surgery, I gripped Michael and the anaesthetist's hands so tightly that I was sure the blood would stop flowing! The surgery wasn't painful per se — just incredibly uncomfortable. The tugging and the yanking felt so rough, I felt at times like my body was being lifted off the table; they were pulling so hard in order to get Sammy out. I wondered later whether all caesarean operations felt that rough? Through the whole procedure, I had to keep telling myself to relax, I was so anxious. I can recall looking at Michael and being so very grateful that he was with me and that I could lean on his strength.

At some point during the surgery, Michael noticed Doctor Elaine swap places with the head surgeon, Doctor Dennis. He became concerned but didn't say anything.

Sammy was delivered at 1:14 am on 16 September, 2017. His weight was 915 grams, and he measured 35.5 centimetres long. He was not breathing on his own, but they put him on oxygen to assist with this and whisked him away to the neonatal unit before we even had a chance to meet. It took about another 45 minutes for them to finish stitching me back together and I was then wheeled into the recovery area.

You've kept track
of my every
toss and turn
through the sleepless
nights,
each tear entered
in Your ledger,
each ache written
in Your book.

Psalm 56:8

(The Message)

FOUR

Saturday, 16 September (morning)

I was seen to by a lovely lady in the recovery room. She checked me over and followed routine procedure to ensure I was recovering properly. Michael was by my side when Doctor Dena came in.

Dena advised us that there had been two slight cuts to the back of Sammy's head that had happened during the operation, but it wasn't anything to worry about. She also told us that Samuel wasn't breathing on his own when they pulled him out, so they had put him on oxygen immediately. The staff in the neonatal unit were checking him all over and she asked Michael if he would like to come and meet his son. Excitedly, Michael left to meet Samuel for the first time.

I'm not sure how long he was away for, but maybe 15 or so minutes later, he returned. He told me that Sammy had toes exactly like mine! I laughed. Of all things to notice! Poor child — I have ugly toes.

It must have only been about 10 minutes or so after Michael returned, that Dena came rushing back in. She had a very concerned look on her face, and told us that the cuts to the back of his head appeared to be way worse than they had first expected. It would be best for Michael to come right away. As they raced off together, my brain was still in a fog. I hadn't had a lot of sleep over the last three nights and was still recovering from the effect of the drugs. I began to feel worried. I prayed.

About an hour or so after being wheeled into recovery, I was taken back to my room. Michael came in soon after, his face very serious. He said things were not looking good for Sammy and that he had lost a lot of blood.

A few minutes later, Dena came in and stood at the end of my bed, Michael beside me. She told us that things were not looking good at all for Sammy. Sometime during the surgery, he had sustained two lacerations to the back of his head. One was small but the other was a lot deeper. Both surgeons had commented to Dena that it had been a very, very difficult surgery. She could not give us the specifics, but promised that the surgeons would give us all the details we needed.

At the time of his delivery, they did not realise the seriousness of the cut because he was not yet breathing. Once they put him on oxygen, the blood started pumping around his body, and soon came flowing out of the larger cut. Upon inspection, they realised the cut had gone all the way through the back of his head, into his skull and through a major artery.

As soon as they discovered this, they did what they could to stop the bleeding. Then they stitched the back of his head and glued it. During this time, Sammy lost all of his own blood, and the neonatal staff had to give him two blood transfusions. We heard later that they had even sent the rescue helicopter to obtain more blood from elsewhere around the country.

When they conducted a scan on the back of his head, they noticed that the blood had not stopped and was now putting immense pressure on his head and brain.

Up until this point, being in a state of disbelief, I had held my composure. But when I heard about the pressure on his brain, I started to sob. How could this be happening? I was assured all would be well with my son! It seemed so surreal – was this actually happening? My son! My baby! How did it all turn so bad?

Doctor Dena held back her tears as she continued. They had put him on morphine because, "We do not believe that any child should feel pain." That was at least some sort of comfort to me. How could one so little sustain such pain? I managed to choke out the words between tears, "So you don't think he's in any pain?" She shook her head. They would of course keep monitoring him and do what they could for him, but the outlook was not good. She wasn't sure how long we may have with him and suggested we have his sister brought in right away so she could at least meet him. I sat in disbelief. No! This could not be happening. I hadn't even met him yet! How can we already be talking about his death? This was not true. How could it be true? Was this a nightmare that I would soon awake from?

Dena assured us they would not give up on him and they would keep doing their very best, but that we also needed to be aware of the gravity of the situation and that he may not be around for very long. She added that if by some miracle he did survive this, she wasn't sure what state his brain would be in. Dena was incredibly sincere but I just couldn't believe this was the outcome. She told me that they would wheel my bed into the neonatal unit now, so that I could meet my son.

Michael and I were both in shock. I can't even remember whether it was at this point or later that Michael turned to me and said "God can still do a miracle". I nodded, tears streaming down my face, knowing full well that it would be nothing short of a miracle if my Sammy survived this.

I remember being wheeled in my bed out of the room, down the corridor towards the neonatal unit to meet Sammy. At an intersection in the ward, I looked to my right and recognized the male surgeon who was talking to another staff member. He stopped as soon as he saw me and said to the person wheeling me, "I need to talk to them first."

I was turned around and taken back to my room with Michael and the surgeon following behind. There was a horrible awkwardness as you can imagine, as the surgeon came in and stood beside my bed. His eyes locked briefly with ours and then he quickly shifted his gaze to the floor. From memory, he said something along the lines of "I'm very sorry. This was not the outcome we were hoping for. It was a very difficult surgery."

He may have said more, but my recollections from that day are starting to become vague. I do recall he said that this was not the outcome he had hoped for. He had many pauses between his words, choosing them very carefully and clearly not quite knowing how to articulate what he wanted to say and all that he felt.

I wanted to feel angry at him; I wanted to be furious at him! I should be. Because of him, the chances of my son surviving were fast disappearing. However, since the moment I saw him in the corridor, all I had felt for him was compassion and pity. I felt so very sorry for him. It was obvious the weight of the world was on his shoulders. One moment. In just one tiny moment, his routine had become a moment that could mark and define the rest of his life, in a bad way. One moment.

As he stood there by my bed, head down, shoulders stooped, I waited for Michael to say something. Nothing. Silence. Awkward silence.

So, with every fibre of my being, I opened my mouth to say something that, to this day, I am amazed I had the courage to say. "We don't have any anger towards you. We know this was an accident. We know that you were doing your very best to save our baby. He wasn't going to survive in my womb so we had to get him out, to give him a chance. We all make mistakes and we know it was an accident. We don't feel any blame or anger towards you. We want to thank you for doing your very, very best to save our son."

The surgeon nodded his head and then left the room silently. I turned to Michael and asked "You didn't say anything?" "I couldn't," was his reply. He told me later that he had been furious; he had been beyond angry at the surgeon. In hindsight, he was grateful he didn't open his mouth to say something that he would later regret.

When I think back now to that moment, all I can say is that it must have been God's grace that enabled me to say what I did. I don't know how else I could have found the strength to say that. Not when I had just been told in the last few minutes that because of this man's accident, my son's chance at life was rapidly fading. And then to see him and to basically tell him that I forgave him? Beyond words. Completely beyond my understanding. It had to be God. Only God and His unfathomable love, flowing through me.

I know now that God loves each one of us with a love we will never fully understand. We all make mistakes; none of us are perfect and He loves us anyway. In June that year, I had started on a journey of learning more about the perfect love of my Father in Heaven. I thought I knew His love before this, but I was learning that it is so much greater and deeper than my mind had ever understood, and ever will. This moment, as I was speaking to the surgeon, God's love had flowed through me to a man who needed it so very desperately at this point in time.

Soon I was wheeled back out of my room down the hallway, to meet my Sam. My heart was aching beyond words at the news we had just been given, but I couldn't wait to see him, to hold him close. My son. They pushed my bed right up against Sammy's incubator so I could be as close as possible to him. He had two drips going into his mouth and one into his left foot. He was tiny. So very little. I talked to him, and the nurse, Sandy,[20] encouraged me to touch his other foot through the little round hole in the wall of the incubator. He had the smoothest skin which was quite a reddish-brown, but I realised this was only because he was a newborn. My brain struggled to get around the fact that although he was just brand new and I was meeting him for the very first time, he was also probably not going to live for very long. It just didn't make any sense.

After spending quite some time with him, I was wheeled back to my room, Michael following. It was about 4 am now. We took Dena's advice and called Michael's sister Deborah. He woke her up and explained that Sammy had been born, but that an accident had occurred and he was not expected to live much longer. He asked if she could please wake Layla-Grace and bring her in as soon as possible so she could meet her brother.

Deb was amazing. She and her husband Seta, their daughter Fa'aesea and my mother-in-law Nia, arrived with Layla-Grace within the hour.

---

[20] Name changed to protect privacy

Despite the situation, I could not wait to show Layla-Grace her brother. How would she respond to seeing him? She was a big sister now. We explained to her that he was in a cot that looked like a glass box and that unfortunately he wasn't very well. She was very apprehensive and rather intimidated by all the beeping machines in the room, and seeing the drips attached to her brother. We encouraged her to touch his toes, and after a while she almost forgot her surroundings as she bonded with her little brother.

Michael encouraged Layla-Grace to sing "Moe Moe Pepe" to him, a Samoan lullaby that they had both often sung to Sammy when he had been in my tummy. On a couple of occasions, he had kicked rather strongly, so they always sang it to see if we could get another reaction from him. I think she was a little disappointed that he didn't respond in any way to her singing this time.

The neonatal staff let us stay as long as we wanted to, by his cot, singing, talking to him and praying. When my mother-in-law put her hand into the cot and rubbed the back of his hand, he suddenly moved it. We had not seen any movement before this, aside from his chest rising and falling. We were so happy to see this, and Mum felt so encouraged that he had responded to her.

A little while later, back in the room, Michael was advised by Dena that it may now be best to get all the extended family to come and meet Sammy. It was probably just after 6am and his situation had not changed any. He was not breathing on his own, and more scans revealed that the blood had not stopped flowing out of the artery.

Michael sent text messages to all the family, inviting them to come as quickly as they could, for a chance to meet Sammy. Jeff was the first to arrive, because he lived closest to the hospital. Unfortunately, his wife Eva was still in Auckland for work, and not able to meet Sammy. Everyone else arrived within the next few hours – even Tili, Michael's sister, and her family from Wanganui. They had driven about three hours to be there with us.

While we were waiting to be taken in to see Sammy again with all the extended family, Marissa took some of the nephews and nieces to the hospital shop downstairs. She wanted to buy him a special blanket. When she returned with the blanket, my nieces also gave me a soft toy for Sammy and a card in which they had all written. I opened the card and read what my little niece Leah had written: "Dear Sammy, I am sad you might leave. I really wanted you as my cousin." I burst into tears. I wished with all my being that he could stay with us too.

The neonatal staff arranged to move Sammy to a bigger, private room so as to make enough space for everyone to be able to see him. There were probably about 25 of us altogether! At around 11 am, someone finally came to get us.

The staff asked if I would like to hold him, and I excitedly replied "yes!" They picked him up and laid him very gently on my chest, ensuring all the various drips and cords were not tangled. At last I was holding my son! He had an long-shaped face just like Michael's. I opened his clasped hands and put his fingers around my pointing one. So tiny. He had lots of dark lanugo (baby hair) over his body, and the brown colour of hair on his head was about the same as Layla-Grace's.

I said quietly to Michael, "I forgot how much time you can spend just staring at your baby." He was beautiful and so perfect. I wanted to keep him.

Because it was a small room, Michael's family came in first to meet Sammy, while mine waited in the corridor. Unfortunately, because of his fragile state, no one else except Michael was able to hold him. When my father-in-law bent over to kiss Sammy on the head, he lifted his head and opened his eyes ever so slightly, as if to see who had kissed him! He did the same thing when Marissa's daughter, Arielle, kissed him on the head. He opened both eyes at that point. His eyes were a very light blue colour, almost the colour of mint blue toothpaste.

Tili's husband Pona prayed for Sammy. He prayed for a complete miracle of healing. I knew that at this time, people around the world — thanks to social media — were also praying for a miracle. Michael and I fully believed that God could do it, if He wanted to. But we also knew the severity of his state, and so we asked God that if He would choose to heal our son, that it would be complete. We asked that every part of his body and brain would function 100% as it was designed to. We knew that we were asking God for the impossible, but we had complete faith to believe that if He wanted to, God could perform the impossible on our baby.

My elder brother Ronn finally managed to get a hold of my parents in Indonesia via FaceTime so that they could "meet" Sammy too. One of my most memorable moments during this time was when my sister and I sang "Kami Memuji KebesaranMu" over him ("How Great Thou Art," in Indonesian). My parents joined in over the screen. I have loved singing ever since I can remember, and to be able to finally hold my son in my arms and sing over him, was such a precious gift. Our song was a declaration of faith. A declaration that regardless of the situation with my son, my God was still great. He was still on the throne and in control of everything.

After some time, everybody left and we had a bit of alone time with Sammy. During this time, the surgeon came back to see us. I was holding Sammy while Michael was reclining in a chair beside me, taking in the precious moments we had with our son.

Dennis came in to see how we were doing. Michael told him we were doing okay, then asked if he could hold both the surgeon's hands. Dennis looked a little puzzled but held out both hands to him. Michael took a hold of them, looked right into his eyes and thanked him for doing his best under the circumstances, acknowledging that we knew it had been a very difficult surgery. It wasn't the outcome that any of us had expected but unfortunately it had happened. He carried on to say that we knew it was an accident, but that we forgave him and held no anger or animosity towards him. He went on to remind Dennis that his gift was from God to bring healing and life, not harm or death. "Don't let this one incident be a stumbling block to what God has called you to do. God has given you a gift; use it to bring life," he said.

I was stunned. Such a complete turnaround in Michael in less than 24 hours! I felt *so* proud of him. It was as though my heart would jump out of my chest. Dennis, overcome by emotion at

Michael's words, turned his back to us and sobbed back tears. He looked back at Michael and managed to whisper, "thank you." Michael reiterated that God had given Dennis a gift to heal, and to not let this incident stop him from using it for the benefit of others.

After Dennis left, I turned to Michael and told him how very proud of him I was. He told me, "That was God!" He felt different. God had given him a peace despite this horrible storm, and through it, he was still able to forgive and bless. There was an incredible sense of peace in the room. It's quite hard to describe. I guess in fact, that the peace wasn't just in that room. He was alive and well, inside of us.

And over the next few hours, days and weeks, that feeling of peace never left us. It filled every part of our beings and carried us through what was to come.

My grace is
all you need.

2 Corinthians 12:9

(New Living Translation)

FIVE

Saturday, 16 September (afternoon)

During the afternoon, I realised that I had been seeing funny images in my eyes. They had been there all day, but because of everything else going on, I hadn't given them much attention. In my left eye I could see a little girl, in a bright orange ring of fire. All I could see was from her shoulders upwards. She had blonde pigtails (certainly not my brown-haired Layla-Grace!) and was running around happily. My right eye just saw bright orange lights. I was rather confused at all this, but again — due to all else around me — I didn't really think twice about it.

Sometime that afternoon, Dena came back to us and suggested we think about our next steps. She said that although the staff had been doing all they could, there wasn't much else more to help improve his condition. He was still not able to breathe on his own and nothing had changed with regards to the blood pressure on his brain. Although they could continue keeping him on life support, it would only be delaying the inevitable.

Around this time, as I was holding Sammy on my chest, he started to squirm and arch his back. We were told that this was the beginning of a seizure. Dena told us that around 12 to 18 hours after the accident, he would start having seizures due to the pressure of the blood on his brain. This broke my heart — as if it wasn't already broken. How could I cope with seeing my baby son have seizures?

I couldn't bear to see my son in this state, so Michael and I talked it over and made the toughest decision of our lives — to take him off life support. I couldn't believe we were having this conversation. It just didn't seem real. But despite how much it hurt to make this choice, we both felt it was the only thing to do. We felt that if God was going to heal Sammy, it would be once the oxygen tube was removed from his mouth. But we were also very realistic about it. We knew that if it wasn't part of God's plan to heal him, then we hoped that God would take him very quickly. What parent can stand the pain of seeing their child suffer? We told Dena our decision to remove the life support system from Sammy.

At this point, someone offered to call in a professional photographer to take family photos. The hospital had a contact who sometimes provided this service for free, for families in such a situation. We agreed to this, so Michael called and asked Debs if she could please dress Layla-Grace in something pretty and bring her back to the hospital for family photos.

Joelle, our lovely midwife, was on duty again. She wheeled me back to my room to freshen up. Marissa and her son Elijah had returned to the hospital at my request with some make-up so that I could look a little bit presentable for our family photos. I hadn't had much sleep in two days and looked a wreck! Michael changed his T-shirt, brushed his teeth, and then we were back in Sammy's room, ready for the photographer.

Sammy was now out of his closed cot and in an open one, so that Michael could give him a wipe-down. The staff had asked if he would like to do this. Layla-Grace soon arrived and she happily held onto the side of Sammy's cot and peered in while he was being washed. By now, she was so besotted by this little munchkin who looked so much like Daddy. She touched his hands and feet and kept kissing them. I have no idea what she was saying, but she was leaning over, talking to him quietly. She was a big sister, finally able to see and touch her little brother, even if only for a day.

After his quick wash and nappy change, Sammy was given back to me for cuddles.

I treasured every single moment that I was able to cuddle and kiss my son. He loved holding onto my finger for security, and this time, he opened his eyes more often to look at us. His left eye was rather bruised from his rough entry into the world, so it was sometimes a struggle for him to open it, but he did try a few times. Once, when Michael was talking to him, Sammy turned his head and opened his eyes as much as he could, to look at his Dad. When I responded to what Michael had said, Sammy turned his little head to look right into my eyes. I'll never forget that moment for as long as I live. It is forever etched in my mind; one of the greatest treasures stored away in my heart.

I knew then that he recognized us, and in hindsight, that is one of the most precious moments I hold on to. He lived; he was alive. We got to hold him in our arms, and he knew who we were. We didn't see his eyes open very much, but when we did, these moments became our most treasured.

The photographer took many family photos for us, for which we are forever grateful. After she had finished, we enjoyed a few more moments together as a family – just the four of us. Layla-Grace soon became bored so she left the room to play with her cousin Fa'aesea, who was waiting with her mum, dad, Marissa and Elijah in the corridor.

For some time, Michael and I took the opportunity to smother our son with all our love, before inviting Deborah, Seta, Marissa, Elijah and the girls back in to say a final goodbye to Sammy.

Soon after this, we told the duty nurse that we were ready to remove the oxygen tubes from his mouth. It was around 6:45 pm when she came and did this. For the first time since I had met Sammy at the beginning of the day, I got to see what his little face looked like without two tubes in his mouth. The staff had used plaster strips to hold them in place, above and below his lips. Without all that covering a part of his face, we had the chance to see just how perfect and handsome he was. Amidst sobs, Michael managed to take just one picture of his gorgeous face.

I can't express adequately in words how I felt when the nurse removed his tubes. Any parent who has been through a similar experience, will know what I'm talking about when I say this. The anguish and pain mixed with the biggest sense of responsibility; such a weight on our shoulders. It's a decision that no parent should ever have to make. Between sobs, we managed to call out to God and say, "Lord, if you want to heal him, now is your opportunity. But if not, then please, take him quickly."

We remembered how Hannah, in the Bible, had asked God for a son.[21] She had made a promise to God that if He should give her a son, she would give him back to serve at the temple for the rest of his life. God heard her prayer and gave her a son. She named him Samuel.

I felt a bit like Hannah. We had asked God for a son and He had given. Our son too, was Samuel — "heard by God". But now we were giving him back to God. We knew that our kids are a gift from God; they are His first, long before they are ours.

We talked about the people who would be meeting him in Heaven – Michael's sister Mafuli, my Nana, his cousins lost much earlier in pregnancies, my dear friend Lydia. I hoped that Lydia would be one of the people who would help raise him in Heaven, as she had been a primary school teacher and one of the most beautiful people I've ever known. I wondered what his entrance to Heaven would be like. Would they be there, waiting to carry him – pass him around, kiss and cuddle him?

We covered him with affection, stroking his hands, his feet, his head. I was so hoping for a complete miracle, but deep down inside I knew it was his time to go. He gasped for air a few times but aside from that and our sobbing, everything was quiet. There

---

[21] 1 Samuel 1:9-11

were no more beeping monitors. It was just a little baby boy with his mummy and daddy. Each time he would gasp, Michael and I would both whisper desperately, "just go son, please – don't hold on. Just go." We wanted to keep him – oh, how we wanted to keep our son! But at the same time, we didn't want him holding onto breath if he was in any form of pain. Our whole beings ached with an ache I can't even describe in words.

Finally, at around 7:50 pm, he took his last breath and then lay very still in my arms. We just cried and cried, my arms around our little boy and Michael with one arm around my shoulder and one around Sammy.

The nurse came in soon after and recorded his time of death as being 8:00 pm.

Layla-Grace came back in and we told her that Sammy was now gone – he wasn't here, it was just his body. He was now in Heaven with Aunty Mafuli and all the others. She touched him and gave him another kiss. I wasn't sure if she quite understood what had happened. Marissa, Debs and Seta came and gave Michael and I both hugs and then left quietly with the girls.

The staff came in and I handed my son's limp body over to them. They told me that they would prep and then bring him in a basket into my room so that he could be near us.

I was very hungry by now but only managed to have two mouthfuls of dinner when we returned to our room, before I fell straight to sleep. I was absolutely exhausted, physically and emotionally. Sometime around midnight I awoke starving and finished my cold dinner, still on my bedside table. I looked over at my husband asleep on the chair and thought back over the unbelievable turn of events of the last 24 hours. Had it all really happened?

When I looked at the trolley table on my right, I realised Sammy was lying there, in a basket. I started to sob uncontrollably. How could this be true? He was alive and kicking so much in my womb just 2 days ago! How could that body in the basket be my dead son? My crying woke Michael who came over straight away. I shuffled over in my hospital bed so he could climb in beside me and we sobbed together. His arms around me gave me strength. I had been trying to be strong for the last two days, quoting Bible verses, praying, believing in faith that all would be well, and now it was all over. I felt a release and just let it all out, not having to be brave anymore. Not at all the outcome we had hoped for, but we still knew God was with us and had never left us. Not for a moment.

Michael asked if I wanted to hold Sammy, but I shook my head no. To me, Sammy was no longer with us. He was gone. He was now in Heaven — alive! To me, the tiny body of a baby boy lying in the basket next to us was just a shell, something that had held my son's spirit and soul. But he was no longer here.

We talked awhile about what we thought he was doing in Heaven right now. Do babies become adults immediately when they arrive there? Or do they remain babies and grow up there? Can they see us? There is nothing written in the Bible about this, but since my son's death, I have thought so much more about Heaven and wondered what it is like.

Joelle came in and gave us both the biggest of hugs. She had tears in her eyes and told us that the entire maternity ward and neonatal unit was shaken by what had happened. Even the staff who were not looking after us, were utterly shocked by what had happened to Sammy. She said that they all felt terrible and so sorry for us. A baby's death in the ward caused by a surgeon's accident just didn't happen. It was completely unheard of!

She checked my blood pressure and told me that it was still very high but that it should start to come down, now that the placenta was no longer in my system. I told her that I was seeing bright lights in my eyes but didn't have any dizziness or headaches. She told me that the bright lights were a result of high blood pressure and that the image I had been seeing of a child was probably hallucinations caused by drugs from the surgery. Joelle would advise the doctors on duty about this and see if they had any advice to give.

After she left the room, Michael and I settled back down and went to sleep. Marissa had very kindly bought me some lavender oil and herbal sleep remedy earlier, so I took them both to help me fall asleep.

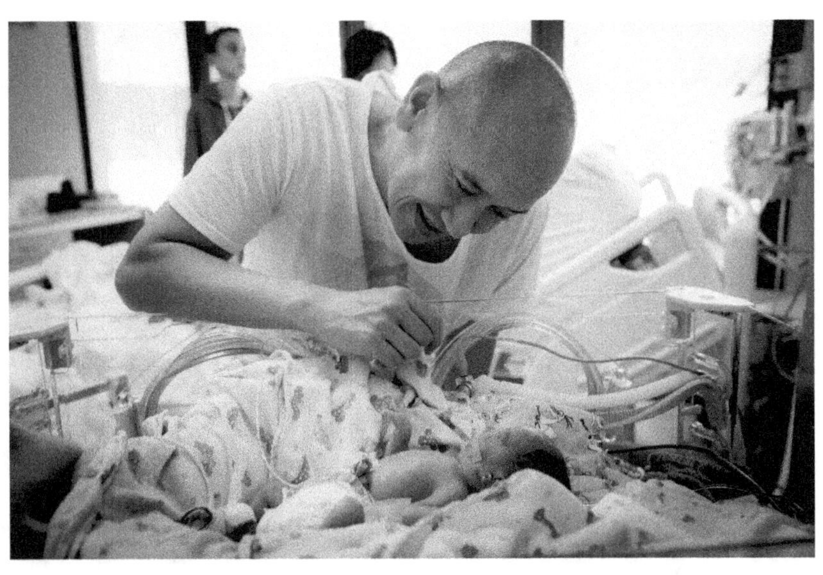

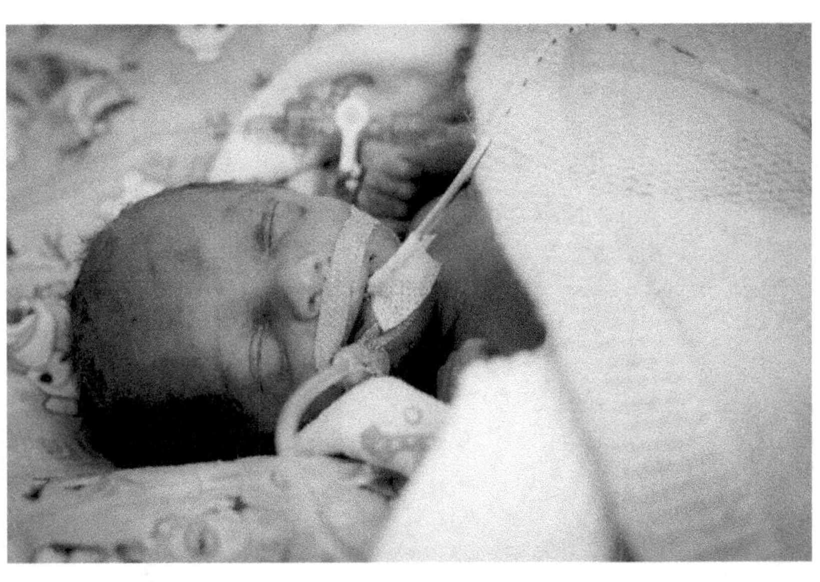

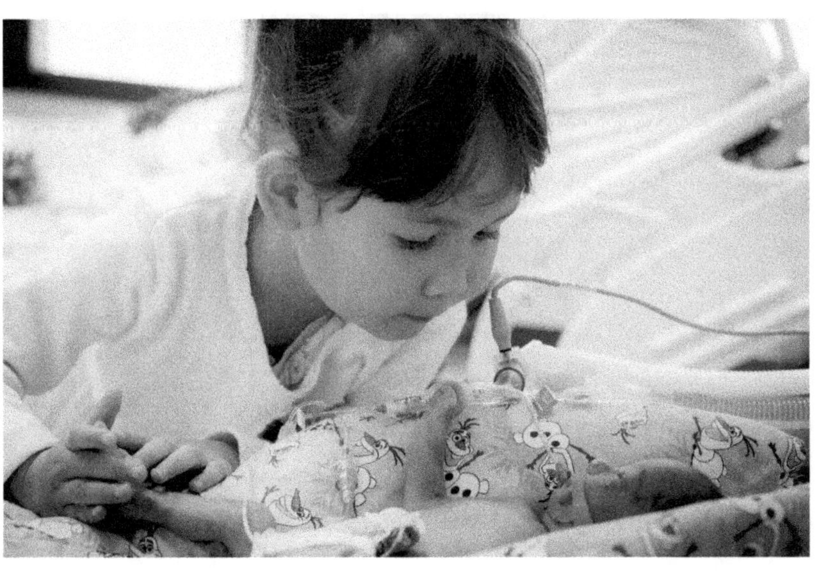

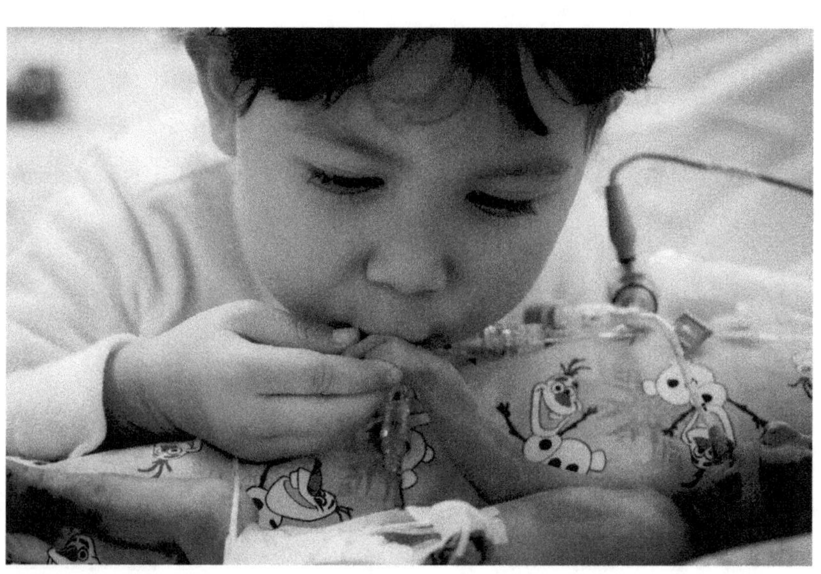

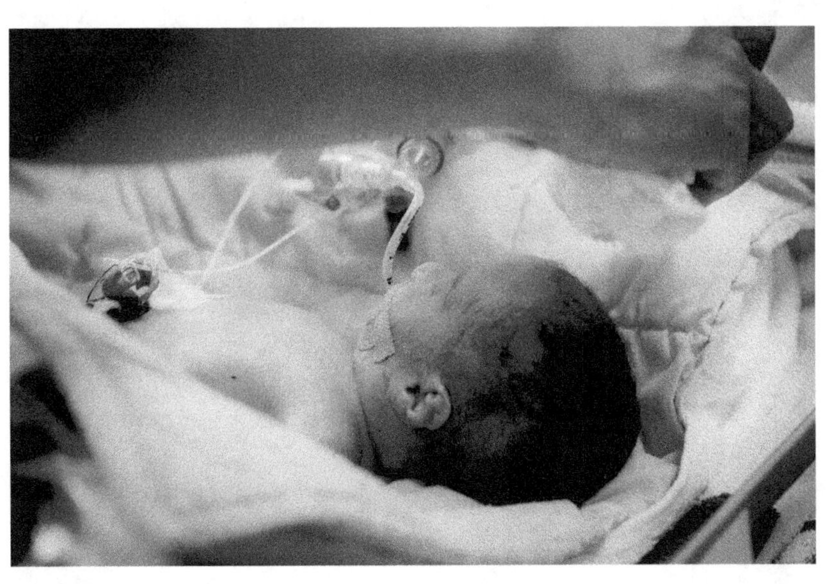

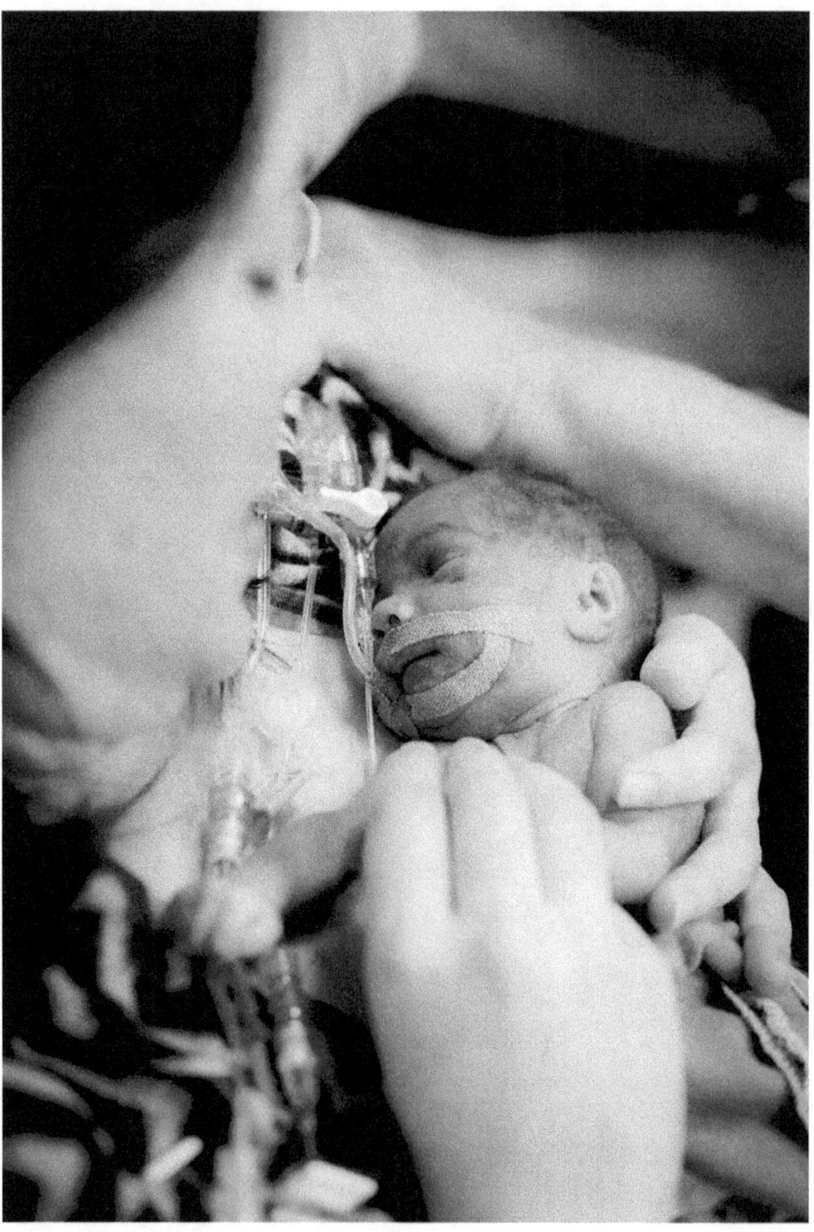

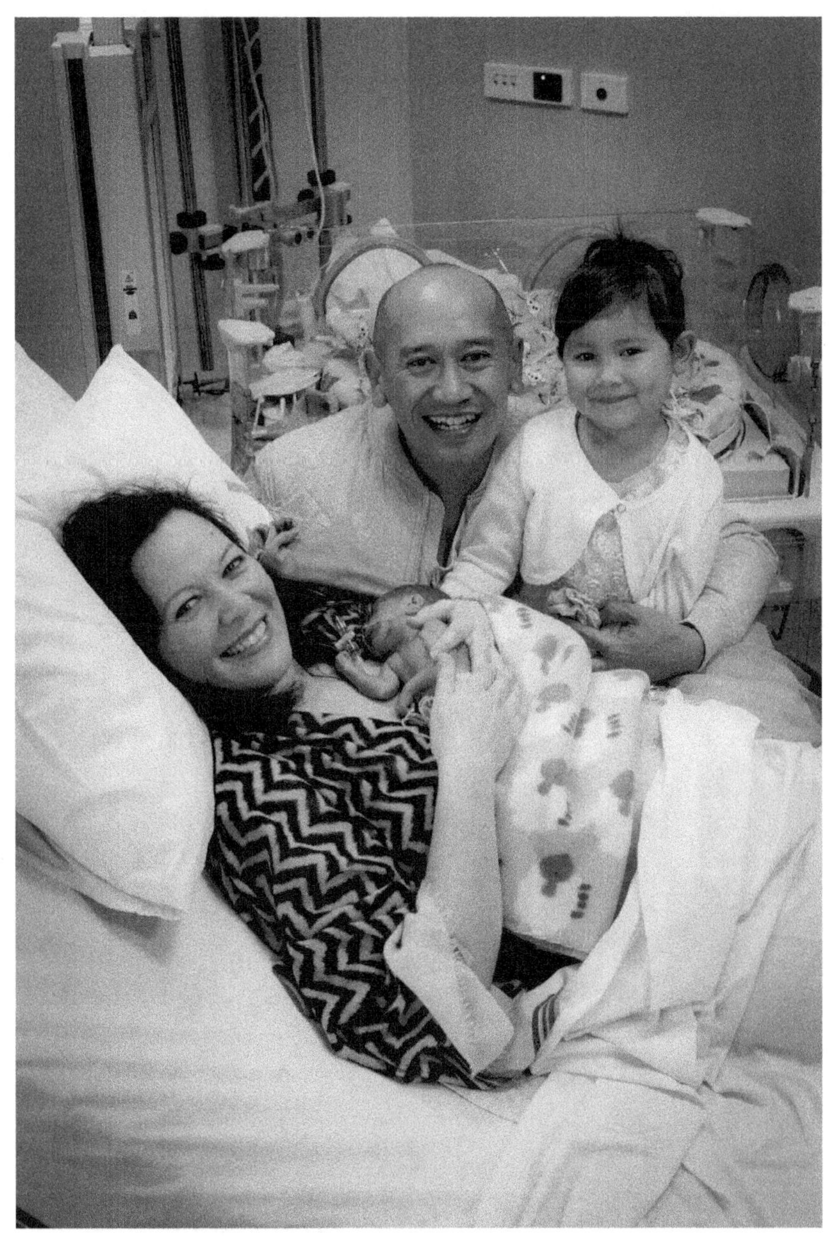

*He heals
the brokenhearted
and binds up
their wounds.*

Psalm 147:3
(New International Version)

SIX

Sunday, 17 September

We were moved to a room at the end of the maternity ward, where we would be a bit further away from the other patients. This suited us very well because it gave us a bit more privacy, being at the end of the hall. It also meant we didn't hear too many of the other babies being born in the unit, which was just too raw for our hearts to bear.

Michael's new bed setup was a big foam unit, instead of a chair. This unit was apparently normally used during labour. We thought that was rather ironically hilarious, despite the tragedy of what we'd just been through.

My body temperature must have been elevated as I was constantly needing the temperature in the room to be made cooler, whereas Michael found it too cool! The staff were so kind to him; they would bring warm blankets from the heating unit whenever he needed them. They also kept offering to make him hot chocolates. I was pleased to see that he was being looked after too. I felt that he had been carrying such a heavy burden on his shoulders over the last couple of days, with everything being so completely out of his control. He had also been slightly overlooked, with all attention having been just on me and Sammy. But I could not have gotten through those last few days without Michael. He is so very strong in his faith in Jesus Christ. Before we had ever met, I was determined to find a man who put Jesus first above everything else. He also had to be kind and be a good decision maker. Over those last few days, he certainly proved that he had every one of those qualities.

The medical staff were concerned with my kidney and liver functions. Both readings were well over what they would normally be, but this was apparently an effect of pre-eclampsia. They were sure these would settle down over the next little while.

Marissa, Ric and their kids came to see us after church that morning, along with Ronn, Rochelle and their girls. It was so nice to have their company. Eden and Leah (Ronn and Rochelle's daughters) wanted to see Sammy's body in the basket beside me, so I let them climb up the side of the tall trolley and peer in. They were interested to talk about his body and Heaven, where he was now living. It was so lovely for me to be able to see how much they loved their little cousin, and to begin to understand that he was now alive in Heaven, even if he was dead on earth.

Some of our pastoral care team from church also come to visit us. They were absolutely shocked when we told them what the cause of Sammy's death had been. They told us that the church service that morning had more attendees than usual, and that one of our young guys had shared an amazing message. Everyone was stunned at our news, but they were all keeping us in their prayers.

Being a small church, normally Michael and I would organize the Sunday services including the band, preaching, etc. But one of our pastoral care team, Mussita, offered to do it for us so that we wouldn't need to worry about it for the next few weeks. She also told us that she and Fay-Lin — another of our amazing pastoral care team members — were organizing a roster of meals for us when we would be discharged from hospital. We felt so loved!

We were also visited by two members of the NZ Police that afternoon. Dena had advised us earlier that due to the nature of Samuel's death, there would be a coroner's investigation. The police would need to be involved and investigate the cause of death. The two police officers did not stay long; they offered us their condolences and told us that they would be making their own investigations which would then be forwarded on to the coroner's office.

After they left, Joelle came in and asked if we would like for her to put a sign on the door saying, "no visitors please." She had seen the number of guests we had received and knew we were drained, still trying to come to grips with everything ourselves. We took her up on the offer and were able to get some rest. She was so amazing to us — the best person who could have been looking after us during this time.

Late that afternoon, after we woke from our rest, we received more guests. Two families from our church came to visit. We were thankful to now be in this larger room that had more space for everyone. It was so great seeing familiar, kind faces. We again shared our story and they prayed for us before leaving.

During this day, we had been given an information pack for parents who suffer the loss of a newborn. We couldn't believe that we now fell into the category of people who had lost a child. Was this really us? We knew that sometime soon we would need to turn our minds to whether to cremate or bury our son. To be honest, we felt overwhelmed with everything and it seemed too soon to be having to think about anything other than just coming to terms with what had happened.

I was incredibly grateful when a friend, Beula, messaged me to pass on her condolences but also offer some very practical advice about funeral homes. A year and a half earlier, she and her husband Kingsley had lost their baby boy to completely unexpected circumstances also. I was, and am, very thankful for friends who have walked a similar path to us. Sharing our grief with them and hearing their experiences has been very healing.

A beautiful young couple from our church, Henry and Chloe, sent a message to Michael to say that if we were interested, they would go ahead and organize for someone to come and make castings of Sammy's hands and feet for us. This was not something I would have thought of, and I believed it would be an amazing keepsake. We were so grateful to them for their thoughtfulness and agreed to let them organize this for us.

Ever since we had arrived in hospital, Michael had been playing worship music to help create an atmosphere of peace and faith in the room. But tonight I asked if he could please turn it off so that I could sleep. I was exhausted, and although I love music and it really had helped to calm me during these last few days, tonight I just needed quiet.

Outside, the rain was falling. It was almost as if God did that just for me. He knows I sleep best when all is quiet and it's raining outside.

Sometime during the night while we were asleep, Dena came in and took Sammy's body away to be investigated by the coroner. She had told us ahead of time that this would happen and that she would be with him for the duration. We were very grateful for her care.

The faithful love
of the Lord never ends!
His mercies never cease.
Great is His faithfulness;
His mercies begin
afresh each morning.

Lamentations 3:22-23

(New Living Translation)

SEVEN

Over the next few days in hospital, Dennis, the surgeon, came to see me every day. Sometimes Michael was with me, but other times he had gone out to do errands. Each visit became less awkward. I can recall telling him, "I pray that you don't feel any guilt from this, Dennis. We know you were only doing your job and that you did your best." Each time Michael or I said anything like this, he was speechless.

He had told us on his first visit that it had been one of the most difficult surgeries he had ever performed. Elaine, the other surgeon who had been working with him to get Sammy out, had said that it was *the* hardest one she had ever performed. I wanted to know what had made it so difficult.

Dennis explained that there had been a few contributing factors. Because Sammy was only 27 weeks and 4 days gestation, my uterus was still very thick and tight, and wasn't stretched as it would be at 40 weeks. So, it had been difficult to cut through the layers to get to him. Also, because of his size, he wasn't yet engaged in place – he was still moving around in my womb. When they conducted a scan just prior to surgery, he was lying one way. However when they opened my womb, he had moved and was lying "transverse" — sideways — across my tummy. Another reason for the difficult surgery was due to the placenta being in an anterior position – in the front of my abdomen, rather than closer to my spine and behind the baby. All these were factors that added up to the difficult surgery.

I guess it was obvious to Dennis that we were Christians, and he asked what church we attended. When I told him that we were the senior pastors of our church, he was rather taken back. He told me that he also was a Christian and that he had moved to NZ only two weeks prior. Dennis wanted to know more details about our church, so I told him. I then went on to say that he would be very welcome to visit us any Sunday. After he left the room, I broke down in tears. I was overcome with very mixed emotions. I had just invited the person whose fault it was that my Sammy had died, to our church! Because church plays such a big role to us, I was basically extending a welcome into our lives, not just a Sunday service. I sobbed and sobbed.

As I look back now, some nine months since Sammy passed away, I can see only God's love and grace through it all. When none of it makes any sense, and I'm a bucket of tears, all I know is that God's love is immense. It is way larger than I ever thought I knew – or will ever really wrap my brain around.

I realise that love truly is a person. I realise that when my Father in Heaven pours His love into our hearts, we can't help but be the people He wants us to be. We become like Him. I'm in no way saying that we're perfect. Goodness no, we are far from it! But when God's love is poured into our lives, it makes us behave in a way which is often contradictory to what comes natural to us. His love takes over and we respond in a way that Love wants us to.

We have had so many people comment, "I don't know how you could forgive that surgeon for what happened." And all we can say is, "it's not us. In our own strength, we couldn't. But God's love flowed into us and through us, responding to an awful tragedy in a way that only *He* could."

I don't think in a million years that we would have had the ability in our own selves not only to forgive Dennis, but to take it a giant step further and bless him! I still pray for him. I know that Dennis has his own story; his own journey to walk through. I know that he too needs healing, peace and restoration. He needs courage. And I pray that his too will be a "God story". That he will come out winning at the other end. Maybe a little battered and bruised like we are, but winning and crying out at the top of his voice that God's love is real. Love is a substance. More than a substance. It is God, Himself. Because God's love changes everything. It changes who we are. It changes how we think, how we see, how we act and how we respond.

My Father in Heaven is love itself. Here is a description of who He is, and how His love transforms us:

"Love is patient and kind

Love is not jealous or boastful or proud or rude

It does not demand its own way

It is not irritable, and it keeps no record of being wronged

It does not rejoice about injustice

But rejoices whenever the truth wins out

Love never gives up

Never loses faith

Is always hopeful

And endures through every circumstance."[22]

---

[22] 1 Corinthians 13:4-7, New Living Translation

How beautiful! These verses have suddenly become so real to me. When I read it and replace "love" with "God," it takes on a whole new meaning.

God's love flowing through Michael and I, keeps no record of the wrongdoing against us.

Of course, I still miss my son! Of course I hurt that I don't have him in my arms, that I'll not be able to see his first steps, feed him chocolate and ice cream, take him to the zoo, take him to sports or music lessons, go on mummy-son dates or carry his children in my arms!

Of course, I have so many unanswered questions. And then, I wonder what I could have done differently that may have stopped – or at least controlled, the pre-eclampsia. But all I can do is trust that God has all the answers. There are days when I have wished things had turned out differently and then my mind turns towards the "what if's." But I have come to understand that this a dangerous place to go. "What if's" only lead to more heartache, bitterness, anger and so on.

In the first couple of days after Samuel's birth and death, Michael and I decided together that our stance on this whole crazy "incident" would be one of forgiveness, grace and trust. We would not allow ourselves to become bitter towards anyone or anything. We decided that, going forward — even when we would have questions — we would not allow them to stay and fester in our minds. That would be one very unhealthy way to live. We want to live healthy, happy lives and we knew that this was a choice. And sometimes it's a very intentional choice we have to make daily.

I know that one day He will answer every question for me. It may not be while I'm here on earth; it will most likely be when I'm reunited with my Samuel. But I know that my God, my Father, is good. I know that His love for me is more than I can ever describe here on paper. I realise that He is not a mean God. The day after Sammy was born, perhaps even that night after we said goodbye to him, I can remember sobbing back tears and saying to Michael, "God's plan is perfect. And even though this makes absolutely no sense to us right now, I still know that God's plans are always perfect."[23]

We have never doubted that God is still sovereign over all, fully in control of every situation. Even situations that are out of our control; we still know, deep down inside, that none of it takes God by surprise. We know that He loves us and has a plan, even when things go awry. "For I know the plans I have for you, says

---

[23] "God's way is perfect. All the Lord's promises prove true. He is a shield for all who look to Him for protection." Psalm 18:30

the Lord. They are plans for good and not for disaster, to give you a future and a hope." Jeremiah 29:11[24]

Fiona Reid, a dear family friend said to me, "Nothing in God's Kingdom is ever wasted." And I know this to be true. God can use every situation — every sorrow, every grief, every heartache – for good. The Bible says, "And we know that God causes everything to work together for the good of those who love God and are called according to His purpose for them." Romans 8:28[25]

He uses everything to work together for our good. Everything – even the ugly moments in life. But it is a choice. We can choose to become hurt, bitter, tormented and victimized by situations — and rightfully so, some would say. But what kind of a way to live is that? Or we can choose to let God's love flow into our lives, constantly, like a running tap. It washes us clean. It changes us from the inside out. We may become a little battered and bruised along the way, but we are clean. We have no stains of bitterness or resentment towards what life throws our way. Michael and I have chosen to live a life free of stains.

During our stay in hospital, one of the songs Michael had on repeat was a song by Lauren Daigle, called, "Trust in You." We

---

[24] New Living Translation
[25] New Living Translation

had heard it several times previously, but the words didn't jump out at me until the day after Samuel's birth, when Michael turned to me and said, "Listen to these words!" They impacted us so profoundly that it only seemed right for us to play the song as part of a clip that Michael put together for Samuel's memorial service, a week later:

"Letting go of every single dream
I lay each one down at Your feet
Every moment of my wandering
Never changes what You see
I try to win this war
I confess, my hands are weary, I need Your rest
Mighty warrior, King of the fight
No matter what I face You're by my side

When You don't move the mountains
I'm needing You to move
When You don't part the waters
I wish I could walk through
When You don't give the answers
As I cry out to You
I will trust, I will trust, I will trust in You

Truth is, You know what tomorrow brings
There's not a day ahead You have not seen

So let all things be my life and breath

I want what You want Lord and nothing less

You are my strength and comfort

You are my steady hand

You are my firm foundation

The rock on which I stand

Your ways are always higher

Your plans are always good

There's not a place where I'll go

You've not already stood"[26]

I love how God spoke to us so much during this season. Whether through songs or Bible verses, or just conversations with people.

Michael had woken up one morning while we were still in hospital, with this Bible verse on his mind: "The faithful love of the Lord never ends! His mercies never cease. Great is His faithfulness; His mercies begin afresh each morning."[27] That evening or the day after, as I was preparing to sleep for the night,

---

[26] **"Trust In You,"** *Written by Lauren Daigle, Michael Farren & Paul Mabury* © 2014 CentricSongs & See You At The Pub (SESAC) / Integrity's Alleluia! Music & Farren Love And War Publishing (SESAC) (admin. at CapitolCMGPublishing.com) / So Essential Tunes & Flychild Publishing (SESAC) (admin. at EssentialMusicPublishing.com)
[27] Lamentations 3: 22-23 New Living Translation

a friend of mine, Rebecca, sent me a text message with the very same verse. She wrote that someone had described God's mercies to her as a 24- hour infusion. When we wake in the morning, God gives us a fresh infusion of His mercies which last for that day. The next morning, we receive another fresh infusion, and so it goes! This verse became our prayer every single morning for the next many days, weeks and months. On the tough days, we would ask God for a fresh measure of His mercies and He would give it. We've come to understand that it gives us the strength to get through another day and has really helped us in our journey of healing.

We were advised by so many around us to just, "Take it a day at a time," and try not to race through the grieving process. We took their advice and would get up every morning, thankful that God would give us the grace to get through that day. One day at a time.

Two days after Sammy's birth and death, my eyesight was still an issue. The left eye in particular, was seeing wavy lines when they were meant to be straight. I was also still seeing flashing lights, although nowhere near as bright as they had been on Saturday. A nurse came to my room to conduct a brief eye exam, but she couldn't find any issues. They scheduled me for an appointment in the hospital's eye clinic on the Tuesday morning. The duty midwife wheeled me down there and Michael accompanied me.

The lady who conducted the initial set of tests didn't seem to be aware of my story. She hadn't yet read my file. I was feeling incredibly weak and as though I would faint at any moment. She was rather nonchalant and I felt as though she was just trying to get through this eye exam so she could move on to the next. I explained that I'd had a caesarean and hadn't been walking around much the last few days, and that I had also lost quite a lot of blood which would probably explain why I was feeling so weak. She rather offhandedly asked me where my baby was, and if he was still in the ward. I was rather taken aback, but managed to let her know that baby hadn't survived. Her whole attitude changed and she became effusively apologetic.

Having completed the first round of tests, I was wheeled back out to the waiting room to await the next. Michael went to get some water for us, and as I was waiting, a young mum came along with her two sons; one in a stroller. She appeared to have her hands full with them. To her, it was just another day and life was just carrying on as per normal. I watched them, and as I did, my eyes rested on the little boy sitting in the stroller, wondering what it would be like to have a son that age. Hot tears started running down my cheeks as the nurse came walking past me.

She saw my tears and realised what was going on. She came over immediately and asked if I would like to wait somewhere a little more private, to which I nodded yes. I felt very fragile.

We ended up being in the eye clinic for three hours and apparently I endured every possible eye test under the sun! The specialist finally concluded that there had been a bit of fluid that had leaked into the back of my left eye. This would have been caused by the very high blood pressure in my head, and resulted in my eyesight being affected. He had conferred with another specialist, and they were both very sure that it would return to normal after a period of a few weeks.

When I did return for my follow-up appointment about five weeks later, my eyesight had almost completely returned to normal. The specialist conducted the same tests on me again and he confirmed that the fluid had completely subsided in my left eye. He also told me that my blood pressure levels must have been extremely high for the fluid to have leaked through. I told him that from memory, the highest blood pressure reading I was aware of was about 170 over 80 or 90. His reply was, "I see people twice your age with those blood pressure readings and none of them have ever had fluid in their eyes." He suggested my blood pressure readings must have been over 200! Even if it had only been that high for half an hour, it would have been long enough to have resulted in the leakage.

When I met with the consultant obstetrician and gynaecologist a week or so later however, she confirmed that my highest blood pressure readings had been 179 at the highest point. She mentioned that it could've been possible that the blood pressure peaked higher between the readings, but it may also have been that the process of pre-eclampsia could have made my blood vessels more leaky than normal. This could have contributed to the fluid leakage in my eye.

After my eye clinic appointment that morning in hospital, I said to Michael that I was hoping to be able to be released that day or the next. It was now Wednesday, and I had been here since Thursday of the previous week. We chatted to the duty midwife and she would confirm with the doctors whether they would be okay to let me go home. They agreed I could go, and before we left that evening, I was given a prescription for a huge supply of various medicines.

Joelle, my amazing caring midwife had come the evening before to say her "goodbye". Her mother in Australia was very ill and not expected to live much longer so Joelle wanted to spend whatever time was left, by her side. It felt like the most natural thing in the world to ask if I could please pray for her. Having just lost my son, I felt her sadness. She was very moved that I prayed for her and her mother, especially in my own time of grief. But I think loss makes you more aware of the sadness of others around you, and I felt a real urge to be able to share the hope I have inside.

Suddenly, I felt very apprehensive about leaving. There had been *so* much change in my life since I had arrived a week ago, and in a way I felt as though I had been in a safe bubble here in the hospital. Everyone here knew our story and had been so caring and attentive to us. To leave these four walls of security seemed very daunting, but I was keen to get home and get better.

Michael and I prayed that we would hold onto the peace we had now, and that as we left and started a new chapter in our lives as a family, we would be more appreciative of each other and those around us. We prayed that we would be more caring and gracious towards people.

It was dusk as we left the city and drove along the motorway towards home. The sun was very low and the sky had a slight pink and orange tinge to it. The last couple of days had been raining, but the sun was out the day I went home. It was so amazing to breathe in fresh air and to be outside again after a week in hospital! It was as if God had painted the beautiful sky just for me.

We got home that evening and Michael helped me settle back in. He would pick up Layla-Grace tomorrow from Deborah's place to allow us one night to unpack everything and get comfortable being back home. I looked around our house and felt very grateful that I hadn't had time to set up anything baby-related as yet. There was no cot to dismantle, no baby's clothes or nappies to give away. The only thing in the house that was in preparation for Samuel's arrival were a few handmade felt clouds and airplanes that Layla-Grace and I had been sewing into a mobile. I saw them lying on Michael's desk, and just cried.

The Lord is close
to the brokenhearted;
He rescues those
whose spirits
are crushed.

Psalm 34:18

(New Living Translation)

EIGHT

We decided to have a Memorial Service for Sammy. At first, I hadn't wanted to do anything. The whole idea of having a funeral or memorial service for my son just seemed wrong. Perhaps I was still coming to grips with the fact that he had gone. I needed to rest and recover and I just didn't want to do anything big. But the more we thought and talked about it, the more Michael and I felt there needed to be some way for us to grieve together with our extended families, close friends and our church family. They had all been part of our journey and it seemed only right to do this.

We organized a service to be held at our church, about two weeks after Sammy had passed away. It was a brief but beautiful service, and our small church auditorium was packed. My brother-in-law Ric, did a wonderful job hosting the service. Michael's strength amazed us all when he led the congregation in singing a couple of songs. I felt so incredibly proud of him! He was so full of hope and faith, it couldn't help but spill over to everyone that was there.

Thanks to my brother Ronn, my parents were able to attend the service via FaceTime. I'm so thankful for technology! It was so nice that they got to "be there" with us. I read Psalm 23, a portion of scripture that had come to mean so much to us in the last few weeks and months. I surprised myself by not falling apart during the reading! The service was short but so meaningful.

We bought 120 helium balloons which we sent off into the sky after the service. I had specifically chosen the colours which we were going to use in Sammy's bedroom – grey, white, baby blue and yellow — the same colours that we had also used to make his mobile with. My father-in-law admitted later that this was the hardest part of the service for him, as it was a symbolic gesture of letting go.

At the morning tea afterwards, we appreciated the chance to catch up with people we hadn't seen in some time. I was exhausted though, and very thankful when Ronn and Rochelle offered to take Layla-Grace home for a play date with their girls. It gave us a few quiet hours at home to just rest.

After Sammy passed away, I had been asking God if He could please give me a vision of what Sammy is doing in Heaven. I just wanted to see how he was, what his life is like there, how old he is, what he loves doing, what his voice sounds like, what he looks like! If I could have one wish granted in life, this would be it.

A day or so after I first prayed this, we were having breakfast at our dining table when Layla-Grace told us that she had dreamt about Sammy the night before! Michael and I glanced at each other and I asked her what had happened in her dream. She told us that she and Sammy had been dancing together to ballet music — her favourite activity. In her dream, she was wearing a pink ballet outfit and he was wearing a black suit. She emphasized a couple of times that he was a one-year-old, but had turned four in the same year. I asked her if she could show me how tall he was in her dream, and she showed us that he was about up to the top of her ear.

There didn't seem to be much else to her dream, but I was amused that they were doing her favourite activity, and intrigued that she said he was one but turned four in the same year. I have no idea how Heaven works, but I'm so much more interested now that I have a son who is growing up there! I know that Heaven doesn't operate by the same time and calendar that we have here on earth, and I sometimes wonder if perhaps maybe,

Sammy is already a year old ... or maybe even four years old, like in Layla-Grace's dream. I am definitely enjoying my time here on earth and I know I have many years left, but I cannot wait to get there and be with my son. I am looking forward to one day having all my family together for the second time.

I did have a dream about my two children, some months later. It was three days before Christmas, the night of 22 December. It was more like a snapshot of them, rather than a dream. In the picture, they were about 2-3 years older than what they are now, so Layla-Grace would have been about 6 or 7 and Sammy looked like he was around 3 years old. I noticed him more than her, probably only because I have such a desire to see what he looks like now. His skin was fairer than her olive skin, and his hair a little darker.

Unfortunately, I didn't see the colour of his eyes though. He had incredibly light blue eyes when he was born, but we knew this would change. We had hoped he would have green eyes like mine because Layla-Grace has her dad's brown eyes. I guess we will find out one day. The dream was certainly more like a snapshot because I didn't know where they were or what they were doing, and there was no further story to the dream. But I was thankful that I got to see a picture of my son with his big sister. I hope and pray that was just one dream of many to come.

I learned very quickly to manage my emotions whenever Layla-Grace was around, because she found it rather unsettling when Mummy would suddenly just start sobbing. Although I realised it was incredibly healthy to let it all out and just grieve, it was also very good for me to have her around. She helped us to not camp out in that frame of mind and to still find fun in our daily routines, despite the grief. In all honesty, it was probably partially because of her that we returned to "life as normal" so quickly. We had to.

One night as I was putting her to bed, Layla-Grace put her arms around my neck, gave me a huge hug and said, "This is for baby, Mum, so you don't have to be sad anymore." Oh, the tears! She carried on, "Cry Mum, just cry." When I asked her why, she replied, "I'll wipe your tears away, Mum. I'll make you feel better." Awww, such a honey. But I realised then that I needed to be strong for her. Such little shoulders were not made to carry Mummy's grief.

They say that children are incredibly resilient, and Layla-Grace certainly was. She came to terms with Sammy's death very quickly. She understood that she had a brother but that he was now living in Heaven and wouldn't be returning to us. She understood that she was still a big sister and always would be, even if her brother didn't live here. I was thankful that she just "got it."

Michael and I soon discovered that we grieve very differently. I really appreciated whenever Michael would give me a heads-up that he was just having "one of those days," so that I knew to give him space. And he learned that sometimes I just need to cry. So, we let each other be. We were both very aware that a death in the family – particularly a child – can put a load of pressure on a marriage. We wanted to be mindful of each other and support each other as best we could through this.

At the beginning, we both found it hard to talk about Samuel without breaking down, understandably. But after a few weeks, I wanted to talk about him. He was very much a part of our lives now. I didn't want to not talk about him as though he never existed. I had carried him in my womb for seven months, in my arms for a day, and now although he wasn't here, he would be in my heart for the rest of my life. I understood though, that Michael still struggled with talking about him, and other people didn't necessarily feel comfortable having me talk about him all the time either. Layla-Grace however, loved talking about her baby brother, so I would bring him up in conversation with her all the time. It seemed to help us both.

Over the next few weeks and months, we had a number of friends talk to us about their journeys of losing a child and how they got through. We came to see just how precious life is and made us want to manage our priorities better! We are so grateful for others who have walked a similar path to us. Just seeing families who are now living full, complete lives despite their loss, gave us hope that we too would get through this together.

About four weeks after Sammy passed away, Michael, Layla-Grace and I went on a small road trip north to Fordell in Wanganui, to visit Tili, Michael's eldest sister. They live in a gorgeous spot out in the country, surrounded by ravines, rolling hills, sheep and deer farms. We celebrated Tili's 50th, which was very bittersweet for us. We had expected to have attended her birthday with Sammy still being in my tummy, but instead he had already come and gone.

We then spent another four days or so at Himatangi Beach, just the three of us. There wasn't much to do down there, which was fine by me! I rested and slept a lot and began journaling, something I hadn't done in years.

When we returned from our little break, I had a follow-up appointment with my GP. She was shocked at what had happened, saying that the surgeons do caesarean operations every day, so how on earth could this have happened? She also mentioned my pre-eclampsia and how odd it was that it had come on so early in my pregnancy. She didn't think they usually occurred till around 37 weeks, and also commented that one doesn't usually get it when they didn't have it in their first pregnancy. These comments added more questions to my ever-increasing list.

I discovered that as I became physically stronger, my emotions began to feel more raw. I felt sadder than I had before, which took me by surprise. I guessed this must have been because I had been focusing all my attentions on becoming better physically. Now that my health was no longer a distraction, my emotions started to surface more. My kidneys and liver were functioning again as normal, my eyesight was improving and I was able to fall sleep without any aids. I was still taking blood pressure medication but this was reducing.

About five weeks after Sammy's death, we started taking Layla-Grace back to preschool. She desperately needed the company of other children. Michael and I enjoyed our days at home, just the two of us. We had been given quite a few seeds, seedlings and plants over the recent weeks, and we found it to be very therapeutic just pottering around the backyard with our plants. God smiled down on us by giving a rare, warm springtime too! This meant we could spend most of our days outside on our deck, in the sun. Just being able to rest while enjoying fresh air and sunshine helped so much.

I felt as though God had given me the gift of time. There was no rush for me to return to work right away. I was still entitled to my full maternity leave of 16 weeks if I felt I needed it. Michael was still without work and we both really felt as though he was not to go looking for anything, as odd as it may sound. Amazingly, we were not struggling financially in any way. In fact, family and friends had been incredibly generous by donating money to us! We were so blown away by everyone's generosity and kindness.

We were in a season of just being able to rest and be in the moment. We had time. We were able to do with it as we pleased, and what a gift that was! One doesn't often receive the gift of time with no agenda. But back in July, before we had gone on our trip to Singapore and Indonesia, Michael had listened to a sermon about rest. We had both really felt like we were going to be entering a new chapter where we would be resting and living by faith. Which is exactly where we were now. We were learning to just rest and "be," and let God provide for us in this season. We knew it wasn't forever; all seasons change. But we really felt that this was the season God wanted us to be in, for now.

I guess one of the many things I learnt over these months is that the key to enjoying life is to recognize the season that you're in and embrace it. Just go with it and give it all you have, whether it is working, resting, being a stay-at-home mum, or whatever. Because no season lasts forever.

At the end of October, we met with Dr Nancy,[28] the consultant obstetrician and gynaecologist who had previously worked with us while I was still in hospital. We asked her many questions and she was able to answer them sufficiently. She confirmed that the hospital was conducting their own review and we would be invited to give suggestions for anything we felt should be included in it.

---

[28] Name changed to protect privacy

He makes me lie down
in green pastures,
He leads me beside
quiet waters,
He refreshes my soul.
He guides me
along the right paths
For His name's sake.

Psalm 23:2-3

(New International Version)

NINE

Psalm 23 had become immensely meaningful to me over this season of our lives. Back in July, when we knew Michael's contract at work was expiring and nothing else was being offered, I had picked up this chapter to read.

I couldn't get past verse 1: "The Lord is my shepherd, I shall not want."[29] I tried to keep reading on, but my eyes just kept going back to this verse. I shall not want. *Not want.* I will not be in want. Regardless of whether my husband's job is soon ending or not, I shall not lack anything. This is what God was promising me. Despite the fact that it appeared as though we were going to be living off next to no income for goodness knows how long, we would not have a need for anything! So, I took that as God's promise to us and wow, did He ever come through. I'll tell you more about that in the next chapter.

---

[29] New King James Version

Verses 2-3 of this chapter became very real to me after I came home from hospital:

"He makes me to lie down in green pastures; He leads me beside the still waters. He restores my soul; He leads me in the paths of righteousness for His name's sake."

People from our church and from Elim Church that I had previously been a part of for many years (pastored by my sister Marissa and her husband Ric), brought us dinners every day for the first three weeks after we returned from hospital. It was amazing. The majority of them didn't just bring us dinner, they brought dessert too. Needless to say, we packed on extra kilos over those weeks! We felt *so* cared for, spoilt and very loved.

During those weeks I felt as though Michael, Layla-Grace and I were living in a bubble. We didn't have to worry about anything – not even what we were going to make for dinner. We could just be together, love each other's company and just be. We didn't even need to worry about the Church, because our pastoral care team were taking care of that. It's not often in life that you get to fully stop and "breathe." But we did. And since then, we have decided to be more intentional about making time to breathe and just be. Sometimes we don't know how to stop and rest, but our Good Shepherd leads us beside peaceful streams. Sometimes we don't even know how to get there, so He leads us. He *makes us* lie down in green meadows and He restores our strength. Some translations say "He restores my soul." The soul speaks of our mind, will and emotions.

It's very easy to keep going along and forget to switch everything off. I know, because I'm so very guilty of that. I'm task-oriented, so I'm driven by my "to-do" lists. I'm a planner. Every day I have my to-do list which is usually a sub-list of a greater list. I love it. I thrive on it. But if I'm not careful, it can also become my focus and steal my attention away from the things that matter more. During this season of recovery, all lists went out the door – I didn't even have a grocery shopping list! God literally made me lie down to rest. I had to stop. I physically wasn't in a great state to get up and about, so I had to rest.

I was "forced" to be list and project-free and it felt amazing. There were no time constraints, nor anything to tick off a list. I didn't need to check my calendar each evening to see what I needed to be doing the next day. I was able to truly rest and breathe.

In fact, this word "breathe" became my new favourite word. I have since become a lot more aware of when projects and lists vie for my attention. I've learnt to let go of them more, in order to give my undivided focus to my family and other far more important things. I've learnt that there's no point in being busy for busy's sake. I'm learning to breathe and enjoy the journey more, with the people I love. I've learnt that money is definitely not everything and that being present with my family is so much more important than what I *do* for my family. I have accepted that the housework can wait and my house doesn't need to be perfect before we have people over. I've learnt to say, "oh well," to stains and spills, less-than-perfect dinners for guests and uncompleted to-do lists.

In short, I've learned that life is too fragile and brief, and that what matters most is people. Letting go hasn't been easy, but it is so worth it! I'm nicer to be around and I don't have such a short fuse a lot of the time. Of course, I'm not talking about a change in personality. God gave me organizational and planning skills for a reason. I'm just learning not to be driven by those things, and to allow space in my life. That's where creativity is birthed and that's when my soul is restored.

The word that kept coming to mind when I thought about those weeks at home with my family, oddly enough, was, "holy". I wasn't sure why I kept referring to that word whenever I thought of those eight weeks after hospital. So, I looked it up. "Holy" means "set apart". We were literally set apart from the routine and busyness of life so that we could rest and just be. And our souls were restored. It was the saddest season of our lives, and yet at the same time one of the most restoring. Because God was with us.

One day we went for a wander around the mall and found a stand-alone hammock on display in a shop. I have always wanted a hammock. Michael said we should just go ahead and buy it. I hummed and hawed … and finally agreed to it. When he asked the sales assistant about the hammock, she said she would go out to the store room and bring out a boxed one from their stock. She returned, scanned the barcode on the box, then told Michael that this was last year's stock and unfortunately it was a black frame (the display one was white). Michael looked at me and I said I actually preferred black anyway. So, he told the sales assistant we would go ahead and buy it. She then told him that the price was actually 75% less than the white one, just because it was black! We couldn't believe it.

We ended up walking out with a stand-alone hammock that was a quarter of the original price! God knew that I needed to rest and that this was something I had wanted for a long time. I felt like He was smiling on us that afternoon. I love it when He does things like that — just because.

"Yea, though I walk through the valley of the shadow of death, I will fear no evil; for You are with me; Your rod and Your staff, they comfort me." Psalm 23:4[30]

For me, this verse became real when I was faced with the idea of surgery, one of my greatest fears. I clung to these words, saying, "I will not fear; I will not be afraid!" I repeated it over and over in my mind to bring peace to my soul. But since Sammy's death, I have felt God's comfort. We have been – and some days still are – walking through the valley of deepest darkness. But He has remained very faithful to us and He has led us through. He continues to walk with us, our hands in His. Knowing who He is, gives us strength and peace.

"You prepare a table before me in the presence of my enemies" Psalm 23:5[31]

It was Thursday night in the hospital, and while Michael slept peacefully, I was anxious. I had struggled with the panic attack earlier and was still so very afraid. Afraid of what was going to happen, afraid for possible surgery, afraid of more needles, I was thinking and meditating again on Psalm 23. Suddenly this verse started to mean something to me. Out of the blue, I felt I heard God ask, "What kind of table do YOU want, Sheryl?"

---

[30] New King James version
[31] New King James version

I thought this was a very odd question to be asked at such a time. But He asked again, "What kind of table do you want?" So, lying there in my bed, I started to picture a lovely, long dining table covered with amazing food … but suddenly I heard God say again, "What kind of a table do YOU want? What do you really want?" So then, of course, I imagined my most favourite "meal" of all – high tea! It was the most splendid high tea with an unimaginable selection of teas and delicious food. A lovely white linen tablecloth laid out with the finest china and silverware. And God was inviting me to come and sit down and enjoy it with Him. He pulled out a chair for me, I sat down and He pushed me back in. He then sat down across from me and we enjoyed afternoon tea together. He had set *my* favourite kind of table with the best of everything, just because He loves me. And not only that, but He was doing this while my enemy – fear – was encroaching all around me. He was inviting me to tea with Him despite the situation. He wanted me to sit down and enjoy time with Him; to enjoy *Him*, even in the midst of my greatest enemy, fear.

God wanted to give me rest and enjoyment, right there, smack bang in the middle of it all. And I realised that *He* is my table. He wanted to be my greatest enjoyment, and He wanted me to enjoy *Him* in the middle of all that goes on around that may threaten and cause me to fear. If I keep my attention on *Him* and let His love pour into my very being, everything else fades into insignificance in the background.

I have often quoted, "Perfect love expels all fear,"[32] but that night, seeing the beautiful table in my mind, I realised what it truly means. When God's pure and perfect love comes in, all fear disappears. When Christ's love fills us up to the brim, there is no longer any room for fear.

What God was doing that night, was pouring His love into me in a way that I could understand (He knows just how much I love my cups of tea!). It was a way that I could truly grasp His intense love for me. In my vision, He came at the peak of my fear, and He pulled out a chair so I could sit down and enjoy the tea, the food and most importantly – Him. I love the Passion Translation of this verse, "You become my delicious feast."

I am learning that any time I am faced with fear, I just ask Him to pour more of His love into my heart and it begins to fade away.

A few days after we returned home, a beautiful young family from our church delivered a care package to us. Inside were so many lovely pampering treats for me, but also food goodies including tea and pastries. Chloe had trawled through my

---

[32] 1 John 4:18, New Living Translation

Facebook page to see if she could find out the things I love. She had specifically driven a rather long distance to one of our favourite French patisseries in the city, to pick up treats for us! I was blown away by her incredible thoughtfulness and attention to detail.

As we were enjoying our stunning pastries, I remembered again this verse. Here we were now, in the middle of our grief, and we were enjoying a beautiful afternoon tea! To me, this again was God wrapping His arms around me and telling me that He loved me.

"Surely goodness and mercy shall follow me all the days of my life; and I will dwell in the house of the Lord forever." Psalm 23:6[33]

Wow. I love this. God's goodness and His perfect, unconditional love – they follow me after me. They follow me! And not just for a season either. No – they follow behind me, *all* the days of my life! Every single day of my life, God's goodness and love are following me. *ME*! I had to repeat this over and over to myself before it truly sank in (yes, I can be a little bit slow in following sometimes). God is so passionately in love with us that He wants

---

[33] New King James version

nothing more than to love on us, *all* the days of our lives. If that doesn't blow you away, I'm not sure what will.

I am so very, very thankful that our family has faith in Jesus Christ. Because we know for certain that we will see Sammy again. No doubt about it. We know that he is in Heaven and he's having a blast. Even though our hearts ache so bad to have him here with us, he is in the best home. And we have the hope that after our lives are over, we will join him – and see our Father face to face, too. How wonderful it is to know that I *will* see my Sammy again, and that I'll get to hold him and smother him with kisses.

About a month or so after returning home from hospital, I was looking for an old book of mine, in a storage box. As I rifled through the box, I came across a book entitled, "God, I need your comfort," by Kay Arthur. The book was all about Psalm 23! I have no idea how such a book had ended up in my collection; I don't remember buying it or having been given it, but here it was. How incredibly timely. I smiled at how God orchestrated that whole moment.

He will wipe
every tear
from their eyes
and there will be
no more death
or sorrow
or crying
or pain.
All these things
are gone forever.

Revelation 21:4
(New Living Translation)

TEN

I returned to work on 14 November, eight weeks after losing my son. Ironically, this was supposed to have been my final week at work before taking maternity leave, and instead I was returning. I felt it was time to go back to work, because although I was enjoying this period of rest, I knew that at some stage I needed to get back to the "real world." I also have a very strong sense of responsibility and knew that there were deadlines looming at my workplace that I needed to be attending to. Although there was still no pressure whatsoever to return, I chose to. But once I made the decision, I had very mixed feelings about it. When I really thought about it, I realised my heart was telling me that returning to work must mean that I was done with grieving and ready to move on. Yet I was far from it! I had to tell myself that grieving was still part of my journey for now and I was not leaving it – or Sammy – behind. I was just adding something else into the mix.

The first day back to the office was very difficult, but I was grateful that many of the staff were away, and I was able to re-enter quietly. Over the next few weeks and months, there were days when I would just be working away at my desk and something would trigger the tears. It is a little ironic that I worked at an early childhood centre! However, I couldn't have chosen a better workplace. Everyone was so understanding and allowed me space and let me talk when I needed to.

Michael was still without work at this point, and still we felt that he wasn't to go looking for work. We were praying that God would bring a job to him, at the right time.

About the second week of December, someone Michael had known from his previous workplace invited him to catch up over coffee. Michael agreed and they met up a couple of days later. Without Michael's prior knowledge, his friend Mark had also invited a work colleague to accompany him to the catch-up. Over coffee, they discussed a new role. Towards the end of the meeting, Michael asked what they wanted of him; did they want his input into the role? A little surprised, Mark's colleague said that they were discussing this particular role because they were offering it to him! Michael was stunned. He walked out of that coffee catch-up and thought to himself, "Did that just happen?"

They not only offered him the job, but they also asked what hours he would like to work, when he would like to start and what salary he wanted. Just as we had asked of God, a job came looking for Michael! Funnily enough, the night before Michael's coffee meeting, Layla-Grace and I had prayed for a job for him and she said to me, "Tomorrow Daddy will get a job!" Gotta' love the faith of a four year old!

We had made it through five months just on my two-day salary and minimal income from our church. Together, they only covered our rent payments. But God had provided not just enough for us to get by over those five months. He had provided more than enough. At Christmas, we gave away more gifts than we had ever done! We wanted to be generous because we felt God had been so generous to us, and we knew He wasn't going to let us go hungry. It was amazing to note that in our darkest hour, God blessed my family more than we could have imagined. "My cup overflows with blessings."[34]

We learned that God really had been wanting to show us that He is our source. Sometimes we rely too much on our own ability to provide for ourselves, but when everything had been stripped from us and all we had was God, He provided more than we could ever have done for ourselves. The income that had been coming in over those months ended the week Michael's job started. How amazing is God!

---

[34] Psalm 23:5 – New Living Translation

Christmas 2017 was definitely a hard one for our family. We missed Sammy's presence. He would have been about 3 weeks old, had he been born on his due date. Originally, I had planned to have a low-key Christmas because of a new-born. Instead however, we hosted my family's Christmas dinner, I had the great privilege of leading the carol singing at Parliament, and I organised our first ever Christmas production at church! This, in addition of course, to the usual Christmas parties and present buying. Halfway through December I stopped and asked myself, "How on earth did I end up taking on so much this Christmas?"

The week just before Christmas, I returned to my doctor's practice for another blood pressure check. The nurse confirmed that it was finally back to normal and I no longer needed to be on medication. Such a great Christmas present!

New Year's Eve took Michael and I by surprise. We were sitting on the couch watching a movie, when Michael turned to me and said, "Happy New Year!" It was midnight. Suddenly a wave of sadness washed over me and I started crying. I felt as though we had left our son behind in 2017. It was a new year, time for new beginnings. But I didn't want new beginnings; I just wanted my son with me in this year, and in all the years to come. But I didn't have him. He would never see 2018 – or any other year – with us. We both sat there, wiping the tears from our eyes, feeling a horrible sadness and emptiness.

Michael's brother Richard gifted us with a holiday in Tauranga, just after New Year. We hadn't planned on having a holiday, but were so grateful for it. As we spent a few days in an unusually wet and stormy Tauranga, somehow God turned my feelings of loss and despondency into anticipation and hope for the year ahead. Something, I think, that only God can do. The Bible says, "We have this hope as an anchor for the soul, firm and secure."[35] Without hope, I don't know how we could get through one day. Hope acts as an anchor to keep my emotions (my soul) firm and grounded. I don't get lost in my despair because I have hope. In the words of the old hymn: "Strength for today and bright hope for tomorrow."[36] I'm so grateful for hope!

Back in September when we had returned home from hospital, everything we had of Sammy's — his few items of clothing, blankets, a couple of teddybears and other paraphernalia — had been packed away. Neither Michael or I could deal with having such a vivid reminder around us all the time. But, as time passed, I wanted to see his photos; I needed to have them around. Slowly, after the new year began, we started to put up pictures of Sammy around the house.

I also felt that it was the right time to pursue my own personal interests. Our church was entering into a new season and I had

---

[35] Hebrews 6:19, New International Version
[36] "Great is Thy faithfulness," Thomas Chisholm

been able to hand some things over to others, so that my plate wasn't as full. Michael too, now had more support with his roles at church. This year, I decided, was the right time to finally write a book and now I had the story.

It feels like a new chapter for our family, and God has given us new dreams to pursue.

Michael and I have had the privilege of sharing our story with so many people. It has changed us. We are not the same people we were before all of this happened. As we have shared our story with others, it has been so encouraging to see a little flame lit in them; whether it is a flame of hope, faith, love, forgiveness or otherwise.

All in all, despite the tragedy of the loss of such a perfect little boy, I have hope. *We* have hope. Hope that we will see Sammy again. Hope that God can somehow use an awful situation for good. Hope for our future, hope that our lives are held in the hands of the One whose love we will never fully comprehend. The hope that life does go on, and that in the ebbs and flows of life, the one thing that remains the same is the unfathomable love of my Father in Heaven.

EPILOGUE

I finished writing this book 2 years ago. It was all ready to go but when it got to the point of getting it published, I hit a wall. Suddenly everything felt too soon and although Michael and I had shared our story with most people who had come across our way, it felt as though now I just wanted to hold everything close to my heart. Perhaps now I just wanted to leave that chapter of my life behind. Perhaps this was how I could keep my baby close – locked away in my heart so I would not lose him again. I felt way too vulnerable to push our story into the big, wide world and I wasn't ready just yet.

For the first 12 months after Sammy's birth and death, Michael and I truly felt carried by grace. Yes, we grieved, but underlying all of that was this incredible sense of God being with us, carrying us. After Sammy's first birthday however, everything changed. It was as though the scaffolding that had propped us up for 12 months was removed and suddenly I had to try and stand on my own. It's not that God's grace ended, but I believe there is grace for a season and that season had come to a close. I had now stepped into a new one where it was time to address a few underlying issues that Sammy's death had brought to the surface. Tragedy seems to have a way of bringing other issues to the fore!

In the time between my finishing the manuscript and Sammy's first anniversary (about 4 months), we had bought a home, renovated it, moved in and Layla-Grace had started school. By September, all of that was over and life settled down to what was, I guess, a new normal.

It was also then, a year after his death, that I discovered a lump in my tummy. I left it for a while but after some weeks when there was no change, I decided I should check it out. My doctor sent me along for a scan which was difficult because I was surrounded by pregnant women and the sound of baby's heartbeats from their ultrasounds. I blinked back the tears. The scan didn't go very well either. The sonographer announced, "this doesn't look normal" and told me she would send the results to my doctor.

The very next day, I had a call from my doctor who scheduled me to come see her as soon as was possible. I saw her the next day. She told me that the scan showed the lump had its' own blood supply and that I should have a biopsy done immediately.

As I left her office, I could see tears in her eyes as she tried to reassure me that not all lumps turn out to be cancerous and that in fact, many of her patients who'd had lumps turned out to be benign. I walked out feeling more shaken than when I'd walked in!

I think that the scare of this, plus the fact that we had experienced a very exhausting few months prior, resulted in me one day collapsing in a heap, absolutely sobbing. I don't just mean sobbing … I mean gasping, pull-your-heart-out sobbing. I was shocked as these emotions had come flooding in out of nowhere, it seemed.

That was September. Because I didn't have health insurance, I had to go on the waiting list to see someone at the public hospital. About a week before Christmas 2018, I was seen to by a specialist at our hospital who asked a few questions, prodded here and there and then told me it was most likely to be an endometrioma and to rest assured it was nothing serious.

This of course, was a huge relief, but I think the roller coaster I had been on with my emotions over the last year finally took its' toll and I suffered from emotional burn-out. Michael had been on his own emotional journey while still keeping his full-time job and running the Church, that he too, nearly burned out.

Around the same time, about a week just before Christmas 2018, we received the coroner's draft investigation. We dreaded opening the letter so we told the coroner's office that we would not open it until after Christmas and our holiday in January. There was no need to put a damper on our celebrations.

At the end of January, Michael and I both took a deep breath, opened the envelope and read the findings. There were a couple of minor details that seemed different to what I remembered but on the whole, it was as we had expected. We responded to the Coroner's office that we agreed with their findings and that we didn't want another hearing to involve the wider family or anyone else.

At the beginning of 2019, I discovered that I didn't like the person I was seeing in the mirror and knew I needed to do something about this. I felt like a shell of a person with no direction, joy or hope. Michael graciously encouraged me to take time off from my responsibilities at Church – I didn't even need to attend Church on Sunday if I didn't feel up to being around people.

"What?" I had argued, "How can I do that? I'm the Pastor's wife! I can't not be at Church!"

I've since come to realise that if you're going to be of any earthly good to anyone, sometimes you actually just have to acknowledge where you're at and look after yourself first. What started as being 2 months off ended up being the whole year away from all Church commitments.

I started seeing a Christian counsellor which turned out to be one of the best things I could've done. She helped me understand how the tragedy of Sammy's death had somehow stirred up all these other issues (unrelated, or so I thought!) that I wasn't aware existed deep down inside of me. Thankfully, by this point, I was strong enough to face these issues and deal with them, one by one.

As I worked through my internal struggles with the help of my counsellor, the Holy Spirit kept reminding me of my Heavenly Father's love all through the lead up to, during and after Sammy's death. Remembering the depth and reality of His love is what kept me going, even in the hardest moments.

The coroner's final decision arrived in the mail in September 2019 – almost 2 years to the day of his death. The conclusion was that Sammy had died of a brain hemorrhage caused by a fatal cut to his head by the surgeon. There would be no charges pressed and the case would be dropped.

Although I had never wanted Dennis to lose his job and felt that any form of compensation would feel like a slap to the face, I somehow felt very let down. To have gone through the heart-wrenching process of having our baby's head investigated the day after his death, to having to relive all those emotions while reiterating our story in detail to the detective just days after .. and to have it hanging over our heads for two years … just for the conclusion to be exactly what we already knew anyway. It just felt like a huge blow. Had all of this been necessary? I don't actually know what outcome I was expecting, but it wasn't this. I felt very flat.

Underlying my discouragement however, was a sense of relief. This was it. There would be no more wondering, no more waiting. Nothing hanging over our heads that felt like unfinished business. Nothing that would keep taking us back to that nightmare of a day two years prior. Well .. almost nothing.

A month later, I was scheduled to have the lump in my tummy removed. I felt terrified again of surgery … one of my greatest fears … and the last time I'd had to face it, the worst possible thing went wrong. So yes, I was incredibly afraid again. But the day before the surgery, I felt an amazing peace fill my whole being and every ounce of fear vanished. The surgery went very smoothly; I couldn't have even planned the day better. We dropped Layla-Grace off to school in the morning, went to hospital, had my surgery and was discharged just in time to pick her up from school. I felt hope that maybe, just maybe, surgeries might not be all that terrible after all.

It was confirmed that the lump was an endometrioma, but they suspected that due its' unusual location, it was a cell that had been misplaced from inside my uterus. This had most likely happened during Sammy's caesarean. I sobbed. Here, again, I felt as though I was being dragged back to that horrible day two years ago that I just wanted to push into the distant past and move on from.

Finally though, I have begun to move on. It's amazing how a heart can heal. I don't believe that time heals all wounds. Not if one chooses to stay in a place of hurt and unforgiveness. No amount of time could heal a broken heart that is locked into one tragic event or moment. I believe that a heart heals when it allows hope in. And this could be a process that takes weeks or months or even years. But a heart that opens up to let hope in – whether it seeps or pours in - is a heart that heals.

Hope is an anchor for our souls[37]; it is what steadies us when the storm rages. Where there is no hope there is despair. As Marilla

---

[37] Hebrews 6:19

Cuthbert in Anne of Green Gables says, "to despair is to turn your back against God" (I just had to throw in a quote from one of my all-time favourites!).

My beautiful mentor Jeannie gave me a very apt description about grief. Grief is like a circle on a piece of paper. In the beginning, the circle of grief fills the entire page. But as time goes by, the piece of paper gets larger. It's not that the circle becomes smaller .. I don't think the pain ever completely goes away … but the world outside of the circle of pain enlarges.

My world since 16 September 2017 has certainly enlarged. I have learned to celebrate with mums who give birth to babies without any complications, have learned to smile when I see a mum playing with her little son and have learned to not feel anxious when walking through hospital corridors. Some days I still struggle, but on the whole, I am doing pretty well because I have a Comforter who wraps His arms around me and tells me to keep on going; He's with me. And I have learned that it's okay to express my emotions and to not keep them bottled inside as if everything is ok when it's really not. I've learned to embrace my humanity and not hold onto the image of perfection.

Can I talk to you, my friend? If you are suffering from a loss of any kind, then I pray that you'll feel God's arms wrap around and hold you so close. I pray you'll know that He cries when you

do, and that He feels what you do too. He is gentle and kind –
He's the best Dad you could ever imagine.

He loves you and wants to walk this journey with you, a day at a
time, giving you hope that this is not the end. I pray you'll know
grace, peace and comfort, in Jesus' name. I pray that you know
His hand holding yours, every minute of each day. I pray you'll
know a love that knows no limits.

And if you've not met my Jesus before, all you need to do is ask
Him to make Himself real to you and He will – He is aching to!
If you have met Him before but have walked away for whatever
reason – hey, He wants you to know that He hasn't forgotten
you and He would love for you to come close to Him again. Oh
how He loves you!

Why don't you pray this prayer:

Dear Jesus

*I've been living life on my own, doing things in my own strength
and I just can't do it anymore. I need You to walk with me and
guide me on this journey of life. Would you please forgive me of
living this life without You and doing things my way? I ask You to
come into my heart and be the Lord of my life.*

By faith right now I receive You into my heart and I receive Your love, forgiveness and grace. Thank You that now You're in my heart, I have hope. I thank You for this new life You have given me, and for Your amazing love that knows no limits. In Jesus' name, Amen.

If you've just prayed this prayer my friend – congratulations! Welcome to the family! I hope you will drop me a line to let me know; I would love to give you a virtual hug and give you some encouragement on your new journey: sheryl@beaconhill.org.nz